What Others are Saying...

Dr. Wishom challenges readers to take a strategic approach to a better lifestyle. By creating your own definition of success, the reader will design a personal blueprint to being the best that they can be and maximizing their human experience. The mind-challenging exercises in the book are useful tools to identify how you can obtain a Fit, Fine & Fabulous life, as well as drawing a clearer picture of who you are and what you ultimately would like to achieve. An exceptional and refreshing read for high achievers!

—Crystal Brown Tatum, CEO
Editorial work featured in national magazines including *Vogue, People, Self, Shape, Health & Fitness,* and *Elle.*
Crystal Clear Communications

Had you not asked me to read *Fit, Fine & Fabulous in Career, Business & Life*, I would not have selected this type of book to read. I must say that it has been an eye-opener. I especially enjoyed all of the tips, techniques, and strategies that you shared in the career and business chapters. Outstanding information! Great read! Awesome book!

—Jeff Reeves, Former NFL Player, Sr. Executive
Founder of AOK (nonprofit), Author: *The Art of Branding Yourself*

Dr. Laureen is a very wise woman who has put her best insights into this thoughtful guide for living life by your own design. She shares deep wisdom from her life experiences and gives you concrete steps to find success on your own terms. If you're a high-achieving woman or an enlightened man with big dreams for your life, Laureen will show you how to live your life at a whole new level through *Fit, Fine & Fabulous in Career, Business & Life.*

—Jan Marie Dore, MCC
The Professional Women's Success Coach
www.janmariedore.com

Dr. Wishom, over the past ten years of being your mentor, accountability and resource partner, I have watched you achieve, grow and become very successful. After reading *Fit, Fine & Fabulous in Career, Business & Life*, I realized that you have truly stepped into your "own exclusive space," and I discovered that I am an "enlightened man" for reading this book. *Fit, Fine & Fabulous* is truly a work of art and a great read for both men and women who want to achieve success in career, business and life.

—Johnny D. Gentry Jr.
Retired Educator, Certified Vocational Supervisor

While other so-called experts pontificate their "expertise" throughout the social media landscape and talk about going to the next level, it is just that—all talk for the most part. Let's be real. How many people do you know who are actually going to the next level? *Fit, Fine & Fabulous* is different! Dr. Laureen is different. She sets her philosophy apart from all the others. Her tools, solutions, and 3R Method are spot-on in helping us define and realize our true intentions and our own individual definitions of success. It is substance-filled, not the superficial.

Dr. Laureen's *Fit, Fine & Fabulous* is an interactive guide that steps us through the process to change our mindset to achieve a "Whole **New** Level." This book is a must-read for the high achiever who aspires to give more, bring more of their unique value to the world, and "get on their own dime." To sum it up, *Fit, Fine & Fabulous* is about authenticity. Dr. Laureen shows us the gems that are necessary to live a life by design and not by default.

> **—Angela M. Petitt, MBA**
> Featured in *Essence* magazine as a "Power Player"
> *Inspirational Woman Magazine*
> International Jetsetter

As Dr. Laureen points out so eloquently in this book, being "successful" is so much more than fame and fortune! If you strive to be someone else's definition of success, you have missed the point and will always wonder why you don't "feel" successful. You must have your own definition of success that comes from within.

She delves deeply into the processes for defining and achieving success. She describes them clearly and succinctly, and generously shares her own journey as a model for the reader. She introduces a cornucopia of techniques that are powerful and effective, utilizing a variety of senses that will appeal to those with various learning styles. This is NOT another rehash of the tired, old exercises of goal-setting and implementation. It is a far richer and more potent resource that gets your imagination in gear and sets your actions in motion. Be prepared to think deeply and act powerfully!

> **—Terri Zwierzynski,**
> Chief Freedom Officer
> www.Solo-E.com

FIT, FINE &
FABULOUS

FIT, FINE & FABULOUS

IN CAREER, BUSINESS & LIFE

THE PROVEN 3R METHOD FOR "GETTING ON YOUR DIME"
AND "TAKING IT TO A WHOLE **NEW** LEVEL"™

DR. LAUREEN WISHOM

MASTERPIECE PUBLISHERS
HOUSTON, TX

This publication is designed to provide accurate and authoritative information with regard to the subject matter covered. It is sold with the understanding that the author is not engaged in rendering legal, accounting, or financial services. If legal, accounting, or financial advice is required, the services of a competent professional person should be sought.

Fit, Fine & Fabulous in Career, Business & Life is a trademark of Dr. Laureen Wishom, Houston, Texas.

Fit, Fine & Fabulous in Career, Business & Life

ISBN: 978-0-9892930-0-6

Published in Houston, Texas by Masterpiece Publishers—a registered trademark of Masterpiece Publishers.

Masterpiece Publishers' titles may be purchased in bulk for educational, business, fundraising, or sales promotional use. For information email: Info@MasterpiecePublishers.com or call 1.281.584.0348.

Library of Congress Control Number: 2013935067

Printed in the United States of America

THIS BOOK IS FOR:

Ellie Hough 6/14
_____

May You Enjoy Your Fit, Fine & Fabulous Extraordinary YOU!

To those who took the time to give an encouraging word, to all who shared a warm, friendly smile and for those who gave best wishes, I dedicate this book to you.

Thank You for Crossing my Path of Life

And May You Be
Fit, Fine & Fabulous in Career, Business & Life™

To Mom, who would have been so proud!

To all the women who want a Fit, Fine & Fabulous career, business and life.

This book is for you!

Special Dedication

Daisy Beavers and Lillie Daniel

With warm appreciation for two awesome women who possess a lifetime of love, knowledge, and experience—over 170 years between the two of them! Thank you, Aunt Daisy and Mother Daniel, for touching my life in such a profound and heartfelt way.

CONTENTS

Foreword xiii

Introduction 1

What is Fit, Fine & Fabulous
in Career, Business and Life? 7

3R Method: Re-Imagine

Building Your W5 Portfolio and Setting Your GPS 11

Taking It to a Whole **New** Level: The Mindset 19

3R Method: Re-Invent

Crafting Your *Strategic Success Plan* 37

How to Fast-Track to Get Your Career on Track 47

Is Your Business Fabulous or Faux? 63

Mastering This Thing Called Lifestyle 83

Built to Last—Positive Relationships 99

Having It All—Being Mentally and Physically Fit 108

Getting in Touch with Your Spiritual Self 121

Money or Wealth—Is There a Difference? 127

Getting Organized and Becoming More Productive 135

Looking Fabulous while Storing Your Wears in Style 143

Fit, Fine & Fabulous Essentials 157

Your Two-Book Portfolio 169

3R Method: Re-Emerge

Taking It to a Whole **New** Level: The Process 173

The Fit, Fine & Fabulous Formula 177

Resources 189

Special Offers. 191

About the Author 199

FOREWORD

It does not matter where we are in life—successful or still struggling, starting a new career or retiring—we all need that extra boost of encouragement every now and then. No matter where you are emotionally, psychologically, financially, or socially, you will be positively impacted by the invaluable principles you will learn by reading this book. You will be inspired and motivated to discover or rediscover who you are and what you are purposed to do. We all can benefit from having a compass to assist us in making destiny decisions. This is what I consider this book to be—a proverbial compass.

Contrary to what you have been told or believe, there are no secrets, magic bullets, or gimmicks to achieving success. *Fit, Fine & Fabulous in Career, Business & Life* is based on the principle that you can shape your destiny once you know who you are and why you were born, you have decided on where you want to go, and you have established clear goals for what you want to achieve.

This book by Dr. Laureen is not just another collection of tips and ideas; it is truly a guide to revamping every area of your life. She has lived every process described in this book and has interviewed over 500 women who wanted to succeed but had at least one obstacle that they thought was hindering their success. She has helped them figure out what really matters and showed them how to transform their career, business and life. I believe she can help you too.

If your dreams and plans appear to have stagnated and your progress is stalled in a holding pattern, don't quit yet. Read on and enjoy the journey as this author takes you on a literary voyage, revealing how she overcame obstacles, fertilized the seeds of her dreams, and designed a vision until she was able to walk into her own Fit, Fine & Fabulous status.

"Re-Imagine, Re-Invent, and Re-Emerge"
into your God-given destiny.

Dr. Cindy Trimm

A best-selling author, high impact teacher, and former senator, she is a sought-after empowerment specialist, revolutionary thinker, and transformational leader. She has earned a distinguished reputation as a catalyst for change and voice of hope to the nations.

Listed among *Ebony* magazine's Power 100 as the "top 100 doers and influencers in the world today," Dr. Trimm is a featured speaker on the world's largest platforms, a frequent guest on Christian broadcasting's most popular TV and radio programs, and continually tops the national bestseller lists. www.cindytrimm.com

FIT, FINE &
FABULOUS

Re-Imagine

Re-Invent

Re-Emerge

Seeing

Practicing

Doing

INTRODUCTION

For over a decade, I have been extremely successful as a Growth * Success * Acceleration Expert. Even with my many successes, I always knew I still had more untapped dreams and possibilities just waiting to emerge.

The idea for this book was conceived in 2009. It was then that I decided to live what has now become the 3R Method: Re-Imagine * Re-Invent * Re-Emerge for achieving Fit, Fine & Fabulous in career, business and life.

I realized that I, like everyone else, was working day-in and day-out to play a bigger game, but I wasn't getting to the next level in the way that I had expected. I realized that I needed to make some radical changes in order to live my life by design.

I'm sure you remember 2009 as one of the worst economic years of recent times. The marketplace became less lucrative, career paths were altered, doors were closed, and the outlook for a fiscal comeback was dim. I watched many people who were riding high or playing a bigger game contend with less revenue, higher costs, fewer clients, and more debt.

It was in those worst of times that I knew that those who were spouting the "playing a bigger game" philosophy or even the ones that focused on the "take it to the next level" philosophy were recommending viewpoints that were no longer viable. The economy as we had known it had changed forever.

In what has now become the "new economy," these dated philosophies won't pave the way to massive revenue acceleration, long-term business growth, or long-awaited career success for entrepreneurs, business owners, career professionals, coaches, and service providers.

The Light Bulb Moment

Finally my light bulb came on; I understood that playing a bigger game put me into the "me too" category. Taking it to the next level was just another way of saying, "Now climb to the next rung on the ladder." All of sudden, this thinking was just too small.

Why would I want to be a "me too" person, and why would I only want to climb one rung at a time?

My new insight was that I wanted to live an extreme life by my own design. So I abandoned the "play a bigger game" and "take it to the next level" values and decided to operate from a place that I call "Taking It to a Whole **New** Level." I wanted to get "on my dime" once and for all and create my exclusive space.

This new consciousness was eye-opening.

I began to realize that I could do things other than just move up one rung at a time (a.k.a. next-level thinking). I realized that this "Taking It to a Whole **New** Level" philosophy allowed me to think differently, ponder new things, and reflect on things that could be different.

I saw the newness and the expansiveness of what *could be* because my focus was on something that wasn't traditional or expected. When you start the process of "Taking It to a Whole **New** Level," your thinking becomes a combination of the "playing a bigger game," "taking it to the next level," "getting on your dime," and "claiming your exclusive space" beliefs on steroids.

Through the 3R Method, I have learned that there are no secrets and no magic pills, but there are formulas, methods, processes, and structures that lead to **Growth** * **Success** * **A**cceleration. The key is to know what the formulas, methods, processes, and structures are that generate massive growth and success.

The outcome of this method is achieving Fit, Fine & Fabulous in career, business and life.

What Makes My Heart Sing

As I look back over the last three years of actually living Fit, Fine & Fabulous, I am thankful for the numerous leadership opportunities that have been afforded to me. I have been energized by volunteering with food pantries, senior services, grief counseling programs, ex-offender job-readiness workshops, hospice and respite care programs, and advocating for disabled persons.

Since 1998, Masterpiece Solutions, LLC (my parent company), has donated $10,000 annually to a deserving nonprofit organization. This donation is earmarked for board development and strategic planning efforts.

When I decided to commit to "Taking It to a Whole **New** Level," I knew that I had to also commit to giving back at a **new** level. It's one thing to donate $10,000 in services but another when you give of yourself every week without fail.

Then in January of 2012, I was asked to sit on the board of the Texas Executive Women as the head of the Strategic Planning effort. Wow! Another **New** level. As part of the Texas Executive Women's mission, I am now involved in a program that mentors teen girls and young women who are college-bound.

My Ultimate Dream

Before you become engrossed in reading this book, I would like to share what I now believe will be my height of "Taking It to a Whole **New** Level." It is the day that I cut the ribbon at the opening ceremony of a chain of facilities around the world, designed to provide shelter, mentoring, and job-readiness training for homeless women with children. I believe that no child should ever grow up without the stability of a home.

As I think about my ultimate dream of opening these facilities, I must thank Audrey Hepburn for reminding me: "Nothing is impossible! The word itself says, 'I'm possible.'"

What Defines Success

Success is not gained by defeat
Success does not occur overnight
Success can emerge at any age
Success is working to full potential
Success is courage
Success is lending a hand
Success is not listening to negativity
Success is being positive
Success is living your life instead of the life of others
Success is being proud
Success is overcoming obstacles
Success is striving
Success is listening to your heart
Most of all success is accepting (3)
What you have accomplished

—Alisha Ricks

WHAT IS FIT, FINE & FABULOUS IN CAREER, BUSINESS AND LIFE?

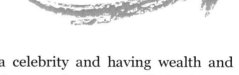

In a world where being a celebrity and having wealth and power is touted as the ultimate end, we can easily be thrown off course and enticed to model ourselves after people we think are successful and powerful.

When we buy into media-generated ideas concerning how we should look (air-brushed), what we should desire (money), and how we ought to define success (job title), we find ourselves copying, competing, and comparing. We try living someone else's life, we envy the talents of others, we covet what some-body else has, or even worse—we judge our "inside" based on someone else's "outside."

What Fit, Fine & Fabulous is Not

Fit, Fine & Fabulous doesn't require you to live by someone else's definition of success. It's never based on the number on your scale, your dress size, your fabulous shoe collection, or if you do or do not believe you need Botox. It is never the practice of depending on external validation to define your significance or your self-worth.

What is Fit, Fine & Fabulous?

Fit, Fine & Fabulous is a state of being where your career, business, life, emotions, family, relationships, lifestyles, health, spirituality, finances, and even your "within" are all aligned and you are living successfully everyday. It's knowing what gives you true meaning, contentment, and peace of mind.

Fit, Fine & Fabulous is like wearing a custom-made suit. It fits perfectly, the fabric is of the finest quality, it's the right color for accentuating your skin tone, it's accessorized perfectly, and it gives you that "wow" first impression as well as a lasting final impression.

Fit, Fine & Fabulous is living a life by design (your design). It does require you to change. When you live by design, you are living on purpose, with passion and power. It is your path to setting intentions, creating a *Strategic Success Plan,* and then taking extraordinary action to achieve the things that you desire.

Let me put it another way. It is the ability to **R**e-Imagine * **R**e-Invent * **R**e-Emerge. It is having the right attitude + the right plan + the right desire to "Take It to a Whole **New** Level" for an extraordinary YOU.

Fit, Fine & Fabulous is loving who you are—no matter your size, what you look like or don't look like, or where you are in your career or your business—and being willing to make radical decisions to achieve a better you.

The Key to Becoming Fit, Fine & Fabulous

Mark Twain, author and humorist, once said: "The two most important days of your life are the day you are born and the day you find out why."

The key to becoming Fit, Fine & Fabulous is to create your own definition of success and to walk with purpose (your why) in every area of life. When you walk with purpose, you will discover the person you are truly meant to be in your career, your business, and your life.

Success is doing what you love. It is discovering how to have a better career, a better business, a better life, and how to be a better you. Philosopher Dan Dennett once said that success is discovering the secret of happiness and then dedicating your life to it.

Purpose is also a state of being where change is accepted without resistance and you seek to make better choices over an extended period of time. In essence, it is the purest form of you, where you are living with authenticity and realizing all your dreams.

> You've got to be a dreamer. You've got to envision the future. You've got to see California while you're climbing 14,000-foot peaks. You've got to see the finish line while you're running the race. You've got to hear the cheers when you're in the middle of a monster project. And you've got to be willing to put yourself through the paces of doing the uncomfortable until it becomes comfortable, because that's how you realize your dreams.
>
> —Jim Rohn

So, if necessary, put aside all of your doubts and your cynicism that you have read books like this before and nothing changed. Remove your negativity, be open to all possibilities, give yourself the benefit of the doubt, and enjoy the 3R Method to Fit, Fine & Fabulous.

Summary Action Steps—Chapter 1

→ In your opinion, what is Fit, Fine & Fabulous?

→ What else would you add to what Fit, Fine & Fabulous is not?

→ Do you have a definition of success? If so— what is it?

BUILDING YOUR
W5 PORTFOLIO AND
SETTING YOUR GPS

Today, I attended the homegoing celebration (funeral) of the mother of a dear friend. The minister performing the eulogy talked about her love for others, how she was always giving to others, and how she helped so many people during her life.

As he was speaking, I thought about how important it is to effectively utilize the time we have, to channel our energy where it counts the most, and to consistently build resources so that we can achieve all that we are purposed to be. I realized that it is important to know where you are on life's journey so that you can best position yourself for "Taking It to a Whole **New** Level."

After I returned home, I continued to reminisce about my dear friend and her mother, and I remembered three very distinct, major changes in my life. The first major change I will call *the U-turn*, the next was *the Stop Sign*, and the third was *the Off-ramp*.

The U-turn major change occurred when I knew without a doubt that I was going in the wrong direction. I also knew that I needed an entirely new direction that would move me away from where I was and closer to where I ultimately wanted to be.

When you find that you need to make a U-turn, you might

need to turn away from bad relationships, an unsuitable business model that no longer works, bad eating habits, a career that is no longer satisfying, excessive spending, procrastination, or always catering to the needs of others first.

The Stop Sign major change happened when I realized that I had been running on what seemed like a treadmill. I was very busy, my schedule was packed, I was doing lots of things, and it appeared as if I were living the life I desired. But the real truth was, I was overworked, overloaded, and overwhelmed.

I was taking action, yet I was not seeing the results that I anticipated. I recommend that you assess whether you need a Stop Sign major change. If you do, then it is the right time for

you to discover your *Why* and identify your *Who*.

When you have the right information and you do the right things at the right time, you stop doing those things that do not get you closer to your chosen intentions.

The Off-ramp major change took place when I had made tremendous progress in achieving my intentions, but I found myself wondering if there were a better, faster, more efficient way to reach my desired intentions. I had done quite well, but I also knew that I could do better and reach a **new** level.

If you need to implement an Off-ramp major change, it's much like taking the off-ramp on a major highway. You don't need to necessarily stop, you don't need to always make a U-turn, but you need to know how to merge onto the highway again with a well-defined compass that I call a W5 Portfolio.

The W5 Portfolio

Instead of wondering how your career, business, or life will turn out based on U-turns or Stop Signs, it is more advantageous to become the architect of your destiny by preparing your W5 Portfolio.

The W5 Portfolio is the framework that defines the *Why*, *Who*, *Where*, *What*, and *When* of your career, business and life.

W5 Portfolio

WHY

This is where you define the purpose of your career or business and all the other elements of your personal and professional life. It is that big "wow" that is the essence of your very core. It is your life's message.

WHO

This is what your "within" consists of: it's your values, beliefs and habits. It is not based on defining your "inside" by someone else's "outside." It is defining what makes you Fit, Fine & Fabulous "within" and who you are right now.

WHERE

This is where you are now with your current definition of success.

WHAT

This is what you want in eighteen months, twenty-four months, three years, five years, or seven years. It is your definition of future success. There is no limit to what you think you can have. If you can envision it, you can achieve it.

WHEN

This is a defined date or time frame for achieving your success intentions.

In summary, everything starts with the *Why*. It gives meaning and purpose to everything you do. The *Why* is what stretches you and forces you to focus and take action.

Remember what Mark Twain, author and humorist, once said: "The two most important days of your life are the day you are born and the day you find out why."

The GPS

Over the past ten years, the Global Positioning System (GPS) has become a very familiar part of our everyday lives.

We use our GPS to determine exactly where we are and the best course for getting from where we are to where we want to go. To travel the course, we enter our starting address and ending destination, and then we receive directions that lead through a series of turns, stops, and possible detours. We arrive at our destination—provided we keep our momentum, stay on course, follow the directions, and remain determined.

Remember, the starting address is your W5 Portfolio and the destination address is achieving Fit, Fine & Fabulous in career, business and life, based on what you define in your *Strategic Success Plan* (discussed in Chapter 4).

The GPS establishes the course that you travel to achieve success. Another way to think about a GPS is that it is your Grounded Powerful Strength. So by having your starting address (your W5 Portfolio) and the ending address (your *Strategic Success Plan*), you can utilize your Grounded Powerful Strength to chart the course to success.

Exercise 2.1
Developing Your W5 Portfolio

Place four sheets of paper before you. Title the first sheet, "My Big Why." Title the second sheet, "Who Am I"; the third sheet, "Where Am I Now"; and the fourth sheet, "What Do I Want to Achieve, and by When."

Before you start this exercise, give yourself a "brain break." Let your brain just relax for 10 to 20 minutes, then get comfortable and spend several hours (or however long is needed) over several days (if necessary) to complete these four sheets.

This exercise is critical to finding your true Fit, Fine & Fabulous self, and it does require some thought and time. Consider it a "brain dump" of who you are as you complete the four sheets.

Keep in mind that your true self does not deny or interfere with your true destiny; it will embrace it. So no matter how uncomfortable this exercise might be, find a way to tap into your inner you to discover who you are—there is nothing more dangerous than denial, especially when it comes to yourself.

Most of the women who have participated in this W5 exercise wanted to write the *How* throughout the exercise process. I had to remind them that the key to developing a W5 Portfolio is not the *How*; it's the *Why*. When you know *Why*, the *How* will follow. The *Why* is the knowledge to get you going, and the *How* is the wisdom that will show you the strategy.

When you know where you are (your definition of success now) and what you want to achieve (your definition of success in the future), it makes it easy to strategically achieve your Fit, Fine & Fabulous.

P.S. If you are having problems with this exercise, try this: We all have what I call an "Inner Board of Directors." An "Inner Board of Directors" is simply a combination of 1) the different aspects of your personality, 2) your knowledge to date, and 3) your past experiences. Many people consult their inner board naturally when they weigh the pros and cons of any situation. So to make it easy to complete this exercise, why not consult your "Inner Board of Directors"?

In summary, you live your Fit, Fine & Fabulous in career, business and life by being strategic, and you live strategically by knowing your W5 and having a fully functioning GPS with a defined destination.

If you want to become Fit, Fine & Fabulous in career, business and life, you can download a complimentary copy of 10.5 Secrets for Achieving Success and Greatness by visiting: www.highachievingwomen.biz.

Summary Action Steps—Chapter 2

→ What did you discover about yourself during the W5 process? Were there any surprises? *Yes*

→ What is your big *Why?* *Smartness INTERESTING*

→ Did you know your *Why* before reading this chapter and completing the exercises? *NO*

Handwritten margin notes:

"Sustainability position with a company in the travel industry" airline, hotel,

• healthy
• going place
• healthy
• meet new people that care
• find my passion
• independence from my job
• be on a board • estab. myself in comm.

What do I want to Achieve and when (4)
respect
recognition
be a wise elder
Known
Successful business
drawing
creative
original
interesting
fun

Where Am I Now (3)
on the edge
close to retirement
searching
on the verge of greatness
• consistent
• steady
• typical

Who Am I (2)
Ellie
black woman
eng
Sr-Citizen
a friend
committed
volunteer
personal
self archeologist
creative
unique
resourceful

My Big Why (1)
I wanted to be smart
I wanted people to look up to me.
I wanted to do something unique
whoooo. interesting

TAKING IT TO A WHOLE NEW LEVEL: THE MINDSET

In Chapter 2, I discussed how to develop your W5 Portfolio and the importance of having a set course to travel (utilizing your GPS). By establishing your W5 Portfolio and using your GPS to determine where you are and where you want to be, you now have the foundation needed to help you focus on "Taking It to a Whole **New** Level."

One of the most important things that I learned throughout this process is how the mind works. With my new understanding of who I was and what I wanted to achieve, I gained control of my thoughts and emotions, rather than the other way around. With this mindset, I am able to live a life by design rather than default.

So after working through my own W5 Portfolio and setting my own GPS, I was positioned to **R**e-Imagine * **R**e-Invent * **R**e-Emerge.

The 3R Method: **R**e-Imagine * **R**e-Invent * **R**e-Emerge is a powerful combination of my own winning formulas and processes and some of the practices that I gathered from high-achieving women I interviewed from all over the world, including entrepreneurs, executives, nonprofit leaders, career professionals, coaches, and service providers.

The Definition of Mindset

According to freedictionary.com, a *mindset* is "a fixed mental attitude or disposition that predetermines a person's responses to interpretations of situations. It is an inclination or a habit. It is a complex mental state involving beliefs, feelings, values, and dispositions for acting certain ways."

Studies show that your mindset drives 90 percent of your success. I believe your mindset is either 90 percent of your success or 90 percent of your failure.

Remember: your mindset drives your actions, your actions dictate your results, and your results lead to success.

Taking It to a Whole New Level: The Mindset

Everything starts with a defining moment and a commitment. For me it was knowing that I had the "within" (inner fortitude and mindset) to start "Taking It to a Whole **New** Level."

I suddenly knew that "playing a bigger game" and "taking it to the next level" were too small. I realized that if I made some life-changing tweaks and became even more committed to following my intentions for maximum results, I would achieve a "Whole **New** Level" Mindset.

I wanted to do some radical things, which meant moving completely out of my comfort zone.

To have a "Whole **New** Level" Mindset you must commit to "doing different things and then doing things differently" (my company's mantra). This is critical. Remember that when you are different, you make a difference.

To attain a "Whole **New** Level" Mindset, you must have the commitment that no matter what, you are going to operate from a "Whole **New** Level." You must have a "do or die" attitude to attain a "Whole **New** Level."

The "Whole **New** Level" Mindset is to have a new vision for the next stage of your career, business, or life. It starts with adhering to the 3R Method: **R**e-Imagine * **R**e-Invent * **R**e-Emerge as your proven method for achieving Fit, Fine & Fabulous. I have discovered that you must become invisible to where you are now and where you have come from.

For me, it was becoming intimately involved in my dreams and hopes for my life. It was that state of getting to know those things that were unknown; it was that moment when I dared to believe in those things that once might have seemed impossible. It was knowing the deepest part of all those "what if" and "if only" thoughts that I've never shared with anyone.

For you, it may be the things that keep you up at night, the things that get you out of bed early in the morning, the things that cause you to ponder relentlessly on how to achieve your desires faster, or those thoughts of "maybe someday" that you just can't seem to let go of.

For me, it was making a radical decision and the commitment that no matter what, more than anything else, I wanted to master the process of "Taking It to a Whole **New** Level."

This process doesn't recognize goals—it only looks at intentions, which are much more powerful.

Start to **Re-Imagine**

Olympic athletes use visualization to perform at their highest potential. They see and feel themselves in the process of their sport's activity from start to finish. According to Albert Einstein, theoretical physicist, "Imagination is more important than science." I am sure that many professional athletes would agree with Mr. Einstein.

Re-Imagine is the first **"R"** of the 3R Method: **R**e-Imagine * **R**e-Invent * **R**e-Emerge. This is how you start.

Re-Imagine is that process of upgrading your self-image (from the inside) through visualization. It is the process of disengaging from the here-and-now of paying bills, taking the kids to soccer practice or tap-dance lessons, or trying to build a better mousetrap so the world beats a path to your business's door.

Another viewpoint is allowing your "within" to imagine life-altering innovations, ideas, trends, and theories. It could be described as the time during which you air out your mind so that you can do some big-idea thinking.

Can you imagine starting to think on those things that are outrageous, unheard of, or even unspeakable? It is that moment when you say, "I don't care what it will cost; I am committed, and I have every intention of investing in myself big-time."

It is the action you do to "Leverage Your Self-Worth for High Net-Worth." It is taking who you are and leveraging it to the highest level of you that you can imagine. It is that state through which you finally "get on your dime."

Re-Imagine is the process of turning on the flashlight and looking deep into your "within" and then discovering those intentions that are based on "Taking It to a Whole **New** Level."

> God's gift to you is more talent and ability
> than you could possibly use in your lifetime.
> Your gift to God is to develop as much
> of that talent and ability as you can in this life.
>
> —Poet Steven Bow

Always know that you have so much "within" that you can't possibly use it up in your lifetime. Your "within" is infinite; therefore, you can be Fit, Fine & Fabulous at any level for a lifetime.

Exercise 3.1
Re-Imagine You

So let's get started. Prepare a cup of hot tea or other relaxing beverage. When I **R**e-Imagine, I love drinking peppermint tea (peppermint tea is good for managing stress). Be sure you have a recording device to record your conscious thought process. Be sure to light a candle. I love the smell of Frutopia (it is a soy candle).

Now close your eyes and imagine that complete darkness surrounds you. Enjoy the darkness and silence for a few moments. Now imagine, in the distance, you can see a shining light. Its source is a beautifully crafted, magnificent lighthouse. Its steady, radiant beams are so bright that you are able to see many things that you have never seen before.

Concentrate on the lighthouse and visualize its light radiating in all directions to allow you to see infinite possibilities and realities for your life.

Begin by looking at yourself three months, six months, one year, three years, five years, and ten years from now. Start by getting rid of the limits you have placed on your "within." **R**e-Imagine is the process of looking at the desired end result from a "Whole **New** Level" Mindset and working your thoughts backwards from there. It includes having the clarity of intention for what you want to achieve in life.

Start to comment out loud on what you see. Be sure to capture every moment on your recording device. Do not rush this experience. Take your time and experience all the possibilities this magnificent light is showing you. After a period of time, let the visualization gradually subside, yet remain within that sense of shining strength.

Take a few deep breaths and stretch your body. Relax for a few moments, and then listen to the recording. You have captured some awesome ideas and mind pictures for what it will take to become Fit, Fine & Fabulous in career, business and life.

I recommend you do this several times over the next two weeks. Get to know your "within" and what success is for you. Allow the **R**e-Imagine to reveal new ways to experience yourself and your life. The next few times that you **R**e-Imagine, do the process without the recording device; instead, make notes and draw pictures of your vision in a notebook.

Remember, you can't touch or feel your future (yet), but you can visualize it.

When YOU Are Different

I always tell people that one of the greatest compliments anyone can give me is to tell me that I am different, because when people are different, they make a difference. When you grasp the process of "Taking It to a Whole **New** Level: The Mindset" you'll be able to make a difference in a big way.

Below is a live-by mantra that I adopted from Wallace Wattles, a "new thought" writer and author. In my opinion, this is the essence of "Taking It to a Whole **New** Level."

I can form things in my thoughts, and by impressing
my thoughts upon formless substance, can cause
the thing I think about to be created.

In order to do this, I must pass from the competitive
to the creative mind. I must form a clear mental
picture of the things I want.

And, I must hold this picture in my thoughts with
the fixed purpose to get what I want, and the
unwavering faith that I will get what I want–closing
my mind to all that may tend to shake my purpose,
dim my vision, or quench my faith.

I am ready to receive what I want when it comes,
and I am acting now upon the people and things in
my present environment.

—Wallace Wattles

Now you see why the first **"R"** in the 3R Method is **R**e-Imagine. It is critical to becoming Fit, Fine & Fabulous.

Mindset Accessories

Much like a great belt, sky-high heels, or a designer bracelet, there are necessary accessories to help you develop a "whole **new** mindset wardrobe." The adorning accessories associated with developing a "whole **new** mindset wardrobe" include:

Setting Intentions
Mastering Clarity
Ensuring Commitments
Practicing Consistency
Achieving Momentum

So let's look at each of these adorning accessories and see how they interconnect and complement your Fit, Fine & Fabulous.

Setting Intentions

Remember there are no goals, only intentions.

Most people are immune to the words *goal* and *resolution*. We use these words loosely and without thought. How many resolutions have you broken, and how many of your goals have never reached fruition?

According to Candace Pert, Ph.D. and neuroscientist, "It all begins with an intention. Intention is higher-consciousness thought. In other words, it's using the mind for a higher purpose—higher meaning—and not limiting yourself to certain outcomes or procedures. When you have intent, you call forth the actual consciousness (awareness) of the universe and therefore have at your disposal all the intelligence contained within it."

Here is the difference between a thought and an intention: an intention is like tying up a care package with string and sending it for delivery to a specified address, while a thought is more like being on the other end of a delivery, with or without knowing the sender or content.

According to Dr. Marcia Reynolds, an international pioneer in executive coaching and author of *Wander Woman*, "When you intentionally transform, you use both your imagination and your self-awareness. You look at who you are being today and what you feel is missing, and then you imagine a broader sense of self that will better serve your aspirations.

"Once you imagine yourself in a different light, you discover what skills and strengths you already have, and then you determine the steps you need to take to fully integrate your new attributes. You mentally see who you want to be first. Then you create a plan for making the mental view a reality."

On my journey, I've found that an intention-based life is always approached with the optimism that gifts are arriving all the time. As the recipient, we are only responsible for signing for the package, unraveling the string, and accepting the gift. This realm of universal consciousness, where everything is potentially an arriving gift, is where infinite creativity lives.

Once mastered, you can move from the first step of the 3R Method, **R**e-Imagine, to the second step of the 3R Method, **R**e-Invent. In essence, you create the intentions to achieve massive results as you **R**e-Invent who you are and what you want to achieve.

You then move to the third step of the 3R Method, **R**e-Emerge, which is defined in detail in Chapter 16. In short, you shift from "playing a bigger game" or "taking it to the next level" to stepping into a whole new realm of "Taking It to a Whole **New** Level."

Your intentions should dominate everything that you do. Your intentions should be so spectacular that you must complete every one of them. When you see intentions in this manner, you will do what it takes to manifest these intentions into success.

According to Bob Proctor, a sought-after speaker and coach, the definition of intention is "something that you are willing to trade the days of your life for."

When I read this, it made me realize that becoming Fit, Fine & Fabulous, which is my ultimate intention, is truly worth me trading the days of my life.

I suggest that your intentions always include: to be authentic and to be balanced in every area of your life.

When intentions are set, you can master clarity around the intentions.

Mastering Clarity

According to freedictionary.com, *clarity* is defined as "the quality of being clear; in particular, the quality of coherence and intelligibility."

Clarity, in a sense, is the key to everything. It's a deep understanding of how the world works and, most importantly, what drives and motivates you. Clarity allows you to act with skill and to be more successful and content.

There is no end to the stories we tell ourselves, the mental gymnastics we put ourselves through, or the truth we try to hide from ourselves. However, possessing radical and comprehensive honesty is the prerequisite for gaining clarity in career, business and life.

When you reclaim your clarity of mind—your clarity of "within"—you unleash all those mental faculties that you developed during your life in a whole new way. It's like cleaning the windshield of your car for the first time. Suddenly, you can see clearly, you can see where you are going, and life becomes more of a pleasure cruise rather than a long, fog-covered drive.

But it's all up to you. No one else can do it for you, and there's no shortcut for mastering clarity.

When clarity is mastered, you are on the fast track to commitment.

Ensuring Commitments

According to dictionary.reference.com, the definition of *commitment* is "the act of committing, pledging, or engaging oneself; a pledge or promise." To commit is to pledge yourself to a certain purpose or line of conduct. It also means practicing your beliefs consistently.

There are two fundamental conditions for commitment. The first is having a sound set of beliefs. There is an old saying: "Stand for something, or you'll fall for anything." The second condition is "maintaining faithful adherence to those beliefs with your behavior."

Possibly the best description of commitment is "persistence with a purpose." This is why it is so important to have a well-defined W5 Portfolio. You simply must know your *Why, Who, Where, What*, and *When*.

The single most important factor for individual success is

commitment. Commitment ignites action. Without commitment, the 3R Method will not work.

I love this saying by John Assaraf, a professional trainer and coach:

> When you are interested,
> You do what is convenient.
> When you are committed,
> You do whatever it takes.

Rick Hansen, author of *Going the Distance,* was in an automobile accident at age 15 and sustained a spinal cord injury that left him paralyzed from the waist down. He became dedicated and committed to raising money for spinal cord research.

To make a long story short, Rick Hansen pushed himself around the world (over 25 months) and raised $23 million for spinal cord research. For me, that's the true definition of commitment: going the distance.

Commitment is the stepping-stone to consistency.

Practicing Consistency

Consistency is a logical order or following of the same pattern. It is unchanging and steady. For example, a person that arrives exactly five minutes early to work every day is consistently punctual. It is being in conformity with a set of rules, guidelines, or policies. It is living or acting in conformity with one's belief or profession.

According to self-help author and motivational speaker Anthony Robbins, "consistency isn't really the sexiest or most exciting word in personal development. But coupled with time, it will give you real results in your life. Sticking with the program and doing something consistently—and not just when you feel inspired or something like that—is very, very powerful."

Surprisingly, doing something every day or nearly every day

is far easier to sustain than doing it once in a while. If you want to be consistent with a new habit, do it every day uninterrupted for a month. Make it an irreplaceable part of your life, not an afterthought that you do occasionally.

Consistency was the turning point in my being able to achieve my intentions quickly. When you have consistency, it leads to momentum, and believe me, the outcomes are phenomenal.

Achieving Momentum

According to freedictionary.com, *momentum* is "the quantity of motion of a moving body, measured as a product of its mass and velocity." Momentum is a commonly used term in sports. If a team has momentum and is on the move, it will take some effort to stop them. If a team has a lot of momentum and is really on the move, it will be almost impossible to stop them.

Momentum can be recognized as "mass in motion." All objects have mass, so if an object is moving, then it has momentum—mass in motion. The amount of momentum that an object has is dependent on two variables: how much *stuff* is moving and how *fast* the stuff is moving. Momentum depends on the variables of mass and velocity.

$$\text{Momentum} = \text{Velocity} \times \text{Mass}$$

Okay, so much for the physics. It isn't easy to build momentum, but once you do, you are unstoppable. You start by taking one small step and one action at a time. When you start, the progress is slow, but once the consistency kicks in, all of a sudden momentum shows up.

You make good choices (**R**e-Imagine), you work your choices (**R**e-Invent), and you implement your choices with consistency (**R**e-Emerge). Remember to start small, take one step at a time, don't stop until the momentum has been built, and keep going once momentum is attained.

Did you know that you will expend ten times as much energy starting and stopping than you spend starting just once and maintaining a regular speed (even if it is a slow speed)?

If you are wondering what adorning accessories to wear to develop a "whole **new** mindset wardrobe," here is the list again:

> Setting Intentions
> Mastering Clarity
> Ensuring Commitments
> Practicing Consistency
> Achieving Momentum

The key to this accessorizing process is to wear all these fabulous pieces everyday. Rest assured—the fashion police will not stop you. The second key is to have fun, enjoy life, and love your "inside" and your "outside" equally.

Remember, the way you see yourself on the inside determines your performance on the outside.

The Wheel of Life

The Wheel of Life describes the segments of our lives. You can use the 3R Method: **R**e-Imagine * **R**e-Invent * **R**e-Emerge in every segment of life to "get on your dime" and "create your own exclusive space."

There should be a balance among all of the segments on The Wheel of Life. Your career and business life should not overpower the other segments.

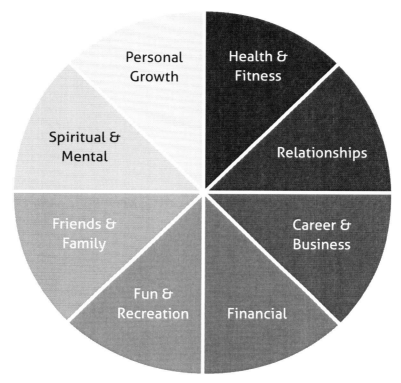

The Wheel of Life

So, before you leave this chapter there is an exercise that I want you to complete that involves the eight segments of your Wheel of Life and another exercise based on your definition of success.

Exercise 3.2
25 Whole New Levels

Prepare a cup of your favorite tea. Relax in a comfortable chair, on the sofa, or on your bed. Don't forget to light a candle. Start by listening to the recordings from Chapter 3, Exercise 1—**R**e-Imagine You.

With a sheet of lined paper in hand, number the lines on the sheet of paper 1 through 25. Draw three columns, and label the first column, "Career"; the second column, "Business"; and the third column, "Life."

In each column, you will write 25 "Whole **New** Level" intentions that you want to have, to do, to accomplish, or to achieve, based on the recording from Chapter 3, Exercise 1—**R**e-Imagine You.

If you do not own a business, list what you want to contribute to the company where you are employed or the intentions for a business you plan to start in the future.

If you are a business owner, you still have a career (e.g., you are a Solo-preneur, Entrepreneur, Thought Leader, Inventor, Community Leader, or Industry Expert), so this column does apply.

In the "Life" column, list those intentions that you want for yourself, your family, and your relationships.

Remember each intention listed must be a Big WOW! Yes, a Big WOW! Remember, the intentions you list must focus on "Taking It to a Whole **New** Level."

The Definition of Success

According to dictionary.com, *success* is defined as "the favorable or prosperous conclusion of attempts for gaining wealth, position, honors, or the like. A person or thing that succeeds."

My father's definition of *success* (and the one I grew up knowing): "Success is getting a good education, a good job, loving others, and always doing those things that take you one step higher."

Wow, that brought back some fond memories.

Exercise 3.3
Your Definition of Success

Relax for a few moments. On another sheet of paper, write your definition of success. You may need to give this definition some thought before writing it.

Summary

Wow, we've covered a lot in this chapter. You've done your W5 Portfolio (Chapter 2); you've completed the mindset exercises; you've discovered your complementary wardrobe accessories (Chapter 3); and now it is time to prepare your *Strategic Success Plan* in Chapter 4.

Based on the 3R Method: **R**e-Imagine * **R**e-Invent * **R**e-Emerge, you have completed the **R**e-Imagine process. Preparing your *Strategic Success Plan* (Chapter 4) is the beginning of the **R**e-Invent process of the 3R Method.

The Masterpiece

It's time to quit waiting for the next big thing to come along before you start—you are the next big thing; you are the masterpiece. You are fully loaded and fully equipped.

Accept that you are a masterpiece. Celebrate who you are and what you have achieved. What should be taking place for many of you is that you can now see how you can "claim your exclusive space" and you are beginning to recognize how to "get on your dime."

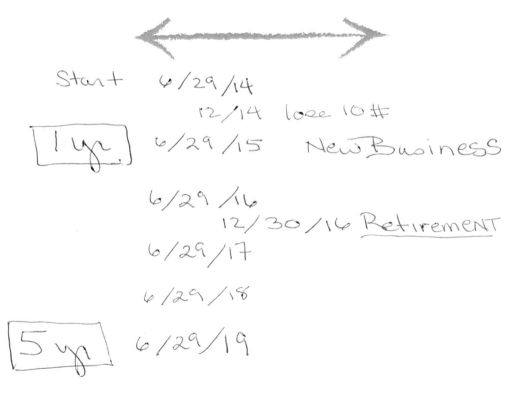

Summary Action Steps—Chapter 3

⟶ Define your mindset before reading this chapter.

⟶ Define your mindset after reading this chapter. Has it improved, is it better, or are you not sure?

⟶ Have you started wearing your adorning accessories yet? If yes, do you like what they have added? If no, why not?

CRAFTING YOUR
STRATEGIC SUCCESS PLAN

I hope that you have enjoyed the first three chapters. Now this is where it all comes together—this is the beginning of the second "**R**" in the 3R Method: the **R**e-Invent process. Before we start pulling it all together, I want to give you the definition of a *Strategic Success Plan*.

A *Strategic Success Plan* is a step-by-step guide that allows you to become laser-focused on what and how to achieve your definition of a Fit, Fine & Fabulous life by design for each segment of your Wheel of Life.

Remember: your *Strategic Success Plan* is a robust document that, over time, produces the outcomes it foretells.

Your *Strategic Success Plan* allows you to see the big picture, plan ahead, and be able to see the many parts of your career, business and life at a micro level. Your *Strategic Success Plan* will help you understand how the many segments of The Wheel of Life relate to one another.

Instead of preparing a twelve-month *Strategic Success Plan,* which is what most people do, I recommend that your *Strategic Success Plan* cover a period of eighteen to thirty-six months. Studies show that an additional six to twelve months will increase your success rate by 90 percent, so I strongly suggest that your *Strategic Success Plan* span a minimum of eighteen months and a maximum of thirty-six months. So every eighteen to thirty-six months, you will modify or create a new *Strategic Success Plan.*

When I originally put my *Strategic Success Plan* together, the personal growth segment had two intentions and the other segments had just one intention. The more I worked on each intention, the more committed I became.

After the first month, I started scheduling more time on my calendar to complete each intention. After a couple of months had passed, I remember saying to myself: "Laureen, look how far you have come in such a short time! Guess what—it looks like you have momentum. Now keep going, and don't you ever stop no matter what—your life really does depend on it."

Every year we all do what is commonly called "spring cleaning," and throughout the year we organize and re-organize our office, workspace, closets, pantry, bedroom, garage, and storage areas. Think of your *Strategic Success Plan* as an evolving plan that charts specific courses for a specific period of time, and along the way you may need to do some spring cleaning from time to time (organize and re-organize based on The Wheel of Life).

Re-Invent, the Second "R" of the 3R Method

The *Strategic Success Plan* is the GPS to **R**e-Invent who you are and what you want to achieve. I can't count the number of times I have had to **R**e-Invent myself during my lifetime. As a result, life has been an amazing and exciting journey for me. If you pay attention to the personal stories of those who are extremely successful, you will notice that they all had to **R**e-Invent themselves at least one time and some, three to five times.

In the new economy, whether you like it or not you will need to **R**e-Invent yourself. Nothing ever remains the same. Without change (**R**e-Invent), your life would be pretty boring, and you will never achieve your Whole **New** Level.

Think about this: every time we add a new dimension to our lives, we gain knowledge, insight, and new experiences. Over the course of a lifetime, this new dimension becomes a deep resource well. There is a richness of wisdom that can only come through experience, and it allows you to **R**e-Invent with more clarity of intention.

I know that embracing change goes hand in hand with seeing life as a journey. When you see life as a journey and not somewhere to get to or something to get through, you are able to **R**e-Invent who you are, change more easily, and have more clarity of intention.

When we **R**e-Invent ourselves, it's like multiplying our knowledge base and perspective. It allows us to consider things from several different angles and perspectives. We don't give up on our former selves; we simply add another dimension to who we are.

Learning how to **R**e-Invent yourself is a journey everyone has to take at least once in his or her lifetime. If it is done correctly and for the right reasons, you'll definitely come out on the other side—a better version of you.

As you prepare your *Strategic Success Plan*, you will begin to see the newness of who you are. You will see the radical shift that you have made in your career, business and life, and you will accept that this is where you will reside. What once was comfortable has now become too small of a dwelling place for you.

Remember, **R**e-Invent is where you feel a bit uncomfortable—and uncomfortable is always good. All successful people attribute their success to doing things that were uncomfortable and facing their biggest fears. When comfort sets in, figure out what you can do to make yourself uncomfortable. **R**e-Invent is always manifested in a state of being uncomfortable.

Exercise 4.1
What Are You, and Why?

This exercise is designed to help you uncover your brand description. On a sheet of paper, write your response to the questions below. Be sure to give some thought to what type of "product" you are and include the justification.

Question 1: If you were a product, what product would you be and why (justification)?

I would be a _Camry_ 7/1/14 _____ (my brand)
because _____ (my justification).

Question 2: Now substitute your name for the brand product you chose and write the justification as a description.

I'm _____ (brand product)
because _____ (justification).

Question 3: List five or six situations where you have received praise. Then list five or six areas of expertise that you possess followed by five or six of your greatest talents.

Question 4: List at least five or six strengths. Don't be shy—list all of them.

Question 5: Write the value that you bring to the world. Don't skip this question because you think you have no value. Re-read "God's Gift" on page 22.

Question 6: Describe yourself in five words or less.

Now that wasn't so painful, was it?

Everyone has a talent. What is rare is the courage to
nurture it in solitude and to follow the talent to the
dark places where it leads.

—Erica Jong

What Are the Inputs to the *Strategic Success Plan*?

When you understand where you are and where you want to go,
you can prepare and implement your *Strategic Success Plan*
the same way an architect does—by working backward from a
vision of the completed structure.

In order to complete your *Strategic Success Plan*, first start
with all of the information from each of the exercises that
you've completed so far, including:

Exercise 2.1—Develop Your W5 Portfolio
Exercise 3.1—**R**e-Imagine You
Exercise 3.2—25 Whole **New** Levels
Exercise 3.3—Your Definition of Success
Exercise 4.1—What Are You, and Why?

Now let's talk about how space, volume, and texture will
enhance the information you've derived from these exercises.

What Are the Space, Volume, and Texture of Your *Strategic Success Plan?*

There are women who enjoy having a lot of space for their
clothes, shoes, and accessories. Many of us are knowledgeable
about textures when making our clothing purchases, and some
of us want to see volumes of shoes in our closets.

When preparing your *Strategic Success Plan*, you should
also be aware of the space, volume, and texture that exist in
your career, business and life.

How will space, volume, and texture affect you? Very simple...

1. Space—this is the staging ground of your destiny. It is your sphere of influence and your place for seizing opportunities.
2. Volume—this is the capacity for introspection, self-knowledge, and intellectual pursuit that you may convey to others (e.g., ideas, understanding, hope, and wisdom).
3. Texture—this is the rich, multi-dimensional quality that includes authenticity, accessibility, and sensitivity.

Your space, volume, and texture will ground you when defining and implementing the intentions defined in your *Strategic Success Plan*.

What Are the Components of a *Strategic Success Plan?*

Before I give you the components of the *Strategic Success Plan*, remember that the *Strategic Success Plan* is your Grounded Powerful Strength (GPS) to **Re**-Emerge (the third **R** of the 3R Method) into your Fit, Fine & Fabulous.

Now, gather together the following information to help you prepare your *Strategic Success Plan:*

- Definition of your Big Why (Exercise 2.1)
- Definition of who you are (Exercise 2.1)
- Definition of where you are now (Exercise 2.1)
- Definition of what you want to achieve and the dates (Exercise 2.1)
- Notes and recordings from the **Re**-Imagine you (Exercise 3.1)

- 25 Whole **new** levels (Exercise 3.2)
- Definition of success (Exercise 3.3)
- What are you, and why? (Exercise 4.1)
- Praises, expertise, and talents (Exercise 4.1)
- Strengths (Exercise 4.1)
- Your value (Exercise 4.1)
- Five words to describe you (Exercise 4.1)
- Include an additional 18- to 36-month vision statement
- Include anything else you need to be more successful
- The intentions for the eight sections of your Wheel of Life, along with what it will take to accomplish them (include completion dates)
- Strategies and tactics for fast-forwarding your intentions
- List of all the opportunities and any possible threats for each intention
- Add your favorite quote and "live by" mantra

When you finish your *Strategic Success Plan,* be sure to sign and date it. Also include the period of time (one, three, five, or seven years) your success plan will cover.

You can also order my *Strategic Success Plan* template and fill in your information (see the Fit, Fine, & Fabulous Products Sheet on page 193).

Strategies for Walking in Your *Strategic Success Plan*

The **R**e-Imagine and **R**e-Invent (the first and second **"R"s** of the 3R Method: **R**e-Imagine * **R**e-Invent * **R**e-Emerge) are the processes of defining, developing, and preparing your *Strategic Success Plan* for living your Fit, Fine & Fabulous life.

The 3R Method allows you to see through new eyes (**R**e-Imagine); to take what you know and re-chart the course

(**R**e-Invent) so that you are in a position to craft a new career, business and life; and then to package it all for implementation (**R**e-Emerge), which allows you to walk in your definition of success.

If your *Strategic Success Plan* is designed for you to walk in flats, then tread the course with ease. If your *Strategic Success Plan* allows you to walk in stilettos, then don't miss a beat. If your *Strategic Success Plan* is designed for running shoes, then sprint the course with grace. The key is to always finish what you start, and that means completing all the intentions that are defined in your *Strategic Success Plan* and to celebrate your "Taking It to a Whole **New** Level."

Your future is where you see the end from the beginning in order to arrive at the intended destination.

My Evolved Definition of Success

In Chapter 3, I defined my father's definition of success. Now that I have lived my *Strategic Success Plan* for three years, here is my evolved definition of success:

"To create ideas and perform activities which have a fulfilling meaning for me and my future intentions. To offer services and solutions that help support people (especially women) and their causes and, in exchange, enjoy positive feelings, monetary and emotional rewards."

The rewards that were generated solely for monetary purposes would never be substantial enough to equal the stamina, courage, and faith that I have gained through the use of the 3R Method.

If my success over the past three years had been measured by the attainment of social status or financial gain, I would be, as my son would say, "the bomb." But in my case, it felt like the bomb exploded inside me, and success as I have come to know it is still not enough to fulfill all of my intentions and God-given talents in one lifetime.

In Summary

Your veritable *Strategic Success Plan* is really a compilation of the dreams (**R**e-Imagine) that you visualized through the various exercises and the intentions that you documented. Now, with a set GPS, you are ready to change (**R**e-Invent) yourself.

With insight and a clear vision, you can examine your current situation, decide where you want to be (**R**e-Imagine), and develop a plan and the best path to get from the start to the finish (**R**e-Invent).

Whether it's your finances, health, fitness, relationships, family, business, or career, if you don't know why and where you are, you have no starting point. Unless you know where you want to be or what's possible, then no matter the path you take, it can never lead you to the life by design you desire.

The heartbeat of this process is the idea that the dreams you have for your life are the dreams life has for you. When your dreams and your life line up, your "within" is poised to **R**e-Emerge.

Don't wait until everything is just right. It will never be perfect. There will always be challenges, obstacles and less than perfect conditions. So what. Get started now. With each step you take, you will grow stronger and stronger, more and more skilled, more and more self-confident and more and more successful.

—Swami Vivekananda

Summary Action Steps—Chapter 4

⟶ How many months will your *Strategic Success Plan* cover, and why?

⟶ How is your *Strategic Success Plan* designed for you to walk through the process? Are you wearing flats, running shoes, or stilettos, and why?

⟶ What is your evolved definition of success? Is it different from Chapter 1's definition? How?

HOW TO FAST-TRACK TO GET YOUR CAREER ON TRACK

When I pondered writing this chapter on the elements of career fitness, many ideas started spinning around in my head. Under the umbrella of career fitness, there is brand fit, technology fit, skills fit, and the list goes on and on.

What I have learned and know for a fact: if you want to accelerate in your career, you must have a Career Transformation Plan. Depending on your strategy, your Career Transformation Plan can be included in your *Strategic Success Plan*, or it can be a complement to the *Strategic Success Plan*.

Getting your career on track is part of the **R**e-Invent (second **"R"** in the 3R Method) process.

Climbing or Leaping–Your Choice

The cornerstone of the "Taking It to a Whole **New** Level" concept for career acceleration is to move from a "climb the ladder" mentality to a "build and leap" mentality.

"Build and leap" is a simple process whereby you build a career ramp (Career Transformation Plan), and then you begin executing your intentions at a faster pace so that you can leap to greater career achievements. Contrast this process with climbing a very tiresome ladder, one rung at a time. "Build and leap" is the best way to fast-track to get your career on track.

Is Your Career on Track?

In this new economy, people must take 100 percent control of their own lives, their own careers, and their own futures. Employees must come to grips with the hard fact that there are limits on how supportive an employer may be. Companies can no longer throw money at people and problems. They are concerned with finding better solutions faster, with fewer resources, to maintain their profitability.

People who struggle to maintain the past or status quo, who cling to an old assumption such as job security, and who resist the inevitability of change are, unfortunately, left behind. Those who catch on and invest in finding and seizing change or new opportunities earn the promotions, recognition, and compensation.

The Japanese call it *kaizen*—the relentless quest for a better way, for higher-quality craftsmanship, and for perfection. The passionate pursuit of *kaizen* improves your competence level and your worth to yourself and others. It also protects your career, even if your company or job disappears tomorrow.

So let's start. If success at a "Whole **New** Level" comes down to just one thing, it may be the art of designing and making strategic career choices. The key is to gather the things you need and then have the courage to let go of what served you well in the past but is no longer valid for your future.

Your *Strategic Success Plan* must include a section describing where you are now and where you want to be in your career in the next one, three, five, or seven years. Your Career Transformation Plan is tailored just for you.

Your uniqueness, experiences, skills, and characteristics extend beyond any one job, any one position, or any one challenge you may be facing. Just remember that you are always bigger than the job, the position, or the career challenges you face.

Just as we sculpt our bodies and exercise to build body

muscle, we must do the same with our career. It's time to start to build and strengthen your career muscle.

Where Does Career Fitness Start?

Career fitness must start with you knowing who you are inside and how you want to look on the outside. This is called your brand. If you don't brand yourself, others will.

Remember, you don't belong to any company for life, and your chief affiliation isn't to any particular function. You are not defined by your job title, and you are not confined by your job description.

The Career Fit Accessories

There are five career accessories that lead to being career fit. To accelerate on the career ramp, you must ensure that the below career accessories are in place:

1. **Think like a brand.** You do not want to be like everyone else. Personal branding is the most effective way to clarify and communicate what makes you different, special, and valuable. Branding is your unique promise of what you offer. Branding is vital to advancing your career. There are many people at your company who may have your same job title. If you do not have a standout brand, you will not get noticed or experience the recognition that you deserve.

2. **Create a standout presence**. Just remember that those who just do their job won't receive many promotions, offers, or opportunities. Those who have created a standout brand and are considered the "go-to person" are on track for career success.

3. **Figure out what you will stand for.** When someone thinks of you, what three points would you like them to remember about you? It's these top three points that will start you on the process of defining your personal brand. If you aren't sure of your top three attributes, or you want to verify that you are on the right track, ask several people (co-workers, peers, or resource partners), and compare their responses with your list.

   Until you stand for something and have a defined brand, you're not going very far in your career.

4. **Recognize that you are the CEO of your career.** Those who have achieved great career success control how they present themselves. They have clearly defined intellectual competencies and have strategically positioned themselves for their next career leap.

5. **Change your career view.** If you see your career as a ladder, you only think about the next rung when a promotion is posted or you are downsized or laid off. When you look at your career as an ascending ramp ("build and leap"), you don't stop and relax; you are constantly advancing to achieve your career intentions.

When you view your career as a ramp to a "Whole **New** Level," you will keep your resume updated at all times instead of when it is needed; you will maintain continual contact with your professional peers as opposed to letting them fade away; and you will seek out tasks and activities that will move you closer to your career aspirations.

Remember, your W5 Portfolio will help you when it comes to defining your brand. Throughout the W5 process and the development of your *Strategic Success Plan*, you will uncover your vision, purpose, intentions, values, and passion for your career.

> The way to get ahead is to start now. If you start now, you will know a lot next year that you don't know now and that you would not have known next year if you had waited.
>
> —William Feather

Brand Attributes

Every brand must have brand attributes. These are the adjectives people use to describe you. Most of the time we are citing someone else's brand attributes without realizing it. For example: "I would like to introduce you to Mary Anne; she is an expert at marketing and social media."

Take a moment and think about how people are introducing you. Do you like their adjectives?

Going forward, spend some time understanding the attributes that people associate with you. You can maximize on the most defining, complimentary, and compelling ones—the ones that help you stand out from everyone else around you.

Knowing Your PBS

When you are career Fit, Fine & Fabulous, you have a well-crafted Personal Brand Statement, or PBS. An effective PBS has three qualities:

- It consists of one, or no more than two, sentences.
- A 12-year-old could easily understand it.
- You are able to recite it from memory at all times.

Be sure to test out three versions of your PBS with trusted colleagues to see which one resonates with them. The best Personal Brand Statements are clear, engaging, exciting, and inspiring. Your PBS should reflect your passion and portray your added value.

A well-defined PBS makes you feel proud and makes you stand out in the career marketplace.

Tips for Getting Ahead:

1. Understand that skills and creativity are king.
2. Don't wait for job assignments—create them.
3. Fly above the radar (if you fly under the radar, you may hear "you're fired," "your position has been eliminated," or "you're being downsized").
4. Make your unique value memorable.
5. Become a specialist—being a generalist is so yesterday.

Tips for Executives and Leaders:

1. Ensure that you have the right people in the right roles.
2. Develop a big footprint view of your role.
3. Redefine how you add value.
4. Overcome the "me" mindset and develop the "us" mindset or "team" mindset.

Building an Unforgettable Presence in a Virtual Workplace

I must tell you a story about my client Mary Beth. Okay, Mary Beth is an alias—the name has been changed to protect the career professional.

Mary Beth is a senior manager at a communications company. Mary Beth and her team have become well known as the "go-to" people for support services within the company.

Recently, Mary Beth was transferred to a new director after a major company reorganization. The director quickly recognized her as a star performer worthy of a promotion, but this required selling the idea to his VP, who had no knowledge of Mary Beth's track record. To make things even more complex, Mary Beth worked from home, managed a small global team, and rarely traveled to the company's headquarters.

Based on the fact that she is a remote worker, here are the five strategies I recommended to Mary Beth in order for her to become visible to internal stakeholders and senior leaders:

1. **Work less.** Too many women make the mistake of thinking that if they just work harder, they will receive recognition. Unfortunately, their reputation is buried under a thankless pile of work. To remedy this, Mary Beth allocated an additional couple hours per week to do activities that made her more visible.

2. **Know your personal brand.** Mary Beth thought deeply about the attributes she wanted to associate with her personal brand. She created a 30-second introduction: "My name is Mary Beth, and I am the Senior Manager of Marketing and Communications. I am responsible for _____. You should come directly to me if you need _____." She used this 30-second introduction to reinforce her brand every time she was introduced to a new person or group inside or outside of the company.

3. **Know who's who in your organization.** With help from an internal mentor, Mary Beth reviewed the company's organization chart and identified the key players and teams that she needed to know. From that point on, she made herself visible to the who's who of the organization.

4. **Create a strategic networking plan.** For every key person on her list, Mary Beth identified a way to

connect with them and build an authentic business relationship. She arrived on teleconferences early to ensure time to talk with each key person. Mary Beth made sure she had talking points to contribute on every teleconference. She set up 20-minute phone calls with key people, scheduled ongoing check-in calls to strengthen working relationships, and invited other managers to present in her staff conference calls (and vice versa).

Mary Beth created a team newsletter to update the stakeholders on monthly milestones within her unit. On the rare occasions that she visited headquarters, Mary Beth leveraged that time by using every available meal or coffee break to meet with key people.

5. **Make your accomplishments visible.** Mary Beth did not want to overdo the self-promotion and make it seem like she was always bragging. As her coach, I pointed out that many women use this excuse to hold themselves back from self-promoting at all. The key is to strike an appropriate balance.

To achieve that balance, Mary Beth prepared short sound bites describing her recent accomplishments and included those sound bites in conversations at every appropriate opportunity. She publicly acknowledged her team (using both "we" and "I" statements) and forwarded the kudos received in emails from stakeholders to her director. She showcased team accomplishments in the monthly newsletter and proactively asked her director, supporters, and mentors to champion her accomplishments to senior leaders.

Six months later, Mary Beth's plan of becoming more visible came to fruition. Every stakeholder in the department knew who she was and the expertise she possessed. The VP commented on how lucky they were to have gained Mary Beth in the reorganization. As a result, she received a promotion.

These are the types of strategies you implement when you want to leap in your career. Notice that they are strategic and well planned and have a definite intention.

Could you use these five steps that I recommended to Mary Beth to build an unforgettable presence in your workplace?

Mentor, Mate, and Mentee

If you plan to succeed in today's marketplace, there are three types of people you must have in your professional life. These people will help you attain your professional aspirations, "build and leap" the corporate ladder, and grow in all areas of your life.

The Mentor will help you reach your intentions much more quickly than you might otherwise expect, and with fewer headaches. You should always strive to surpass your Mentor's current professional level. Don't seek a Mentor for what he/she has earned (i.e., house, car, degrees, clothing, etc.). Seek a Mentor for what he/she has learned (i.e., insight, wisdom, life's lessons, knowledge, and integrity).

Remember, a Mentor is a "learning curve cutter" and a person who shares his/her experiences, knowledge and wisdom. This is your time to receive.

The Mate is a person who will be your career-building partner. The Mate is someone who is close to your age and is in the same career position or close to your career level. The Mate is a person with whom you can exchange ideas, discuss innovative concepts, and receive positive feedback.

The Mate will also experience similar successes and failures. Both of you should leap the success ramp together. This is your time to share.

The Mentee (the correct word is protégé) is a person whom you support by giving them the benefit of your knowledge. The

Mentee looks to you as their Mentor. The benefit of being a Mentor is that the Mentee will compel you to review your life and your accomplishments and will cause you to squeeze out those nuggets that helped you avoid future mistakes and pitfalls. This is your time to give.

The Mentor, Mate, and Mentee make a powerful team. Did you know that the second richest man in the world, Warren E. Buffett, mentors the richest man in the world, Bill H. Gates?

Do You Have What It Takes?

In this tough, competitive job market, you move ahead by building a solid professional reputation as an expert and an achiever. To advance in your career and receive the recognition you deserve, start to:

- Perfect your current skills.
- Learn new skills.
- Demonstrate your value.
- Make outstanding contributions.
- Take on projects that have a significant impact.
- Hold yourself accountable for completing duties proficiently and on time.
- Interact well with others and make viable decisions.
- Admit to mistakes, accept responsibility, and correct any problems immediately.
- Cultivate unique talents that give you a definite edge.
- Be proactive, implement time- and money-saving procedures, and take risks as needed.
- Never let complacency set in or allow your skills to become obsolete.

As you prepare your *Strategic Success Plan*, I know that the information in this chapter will help you craft many awesome intentions for your career.

The PostScript

My sister, Christine Glasco, is an Executive Coach and Leadership Consultant.

While Christine and I have different personalities (I'm, well, extroverted, and she's introverted; I'm passionate about people and their situations, and she's more reserved), we are very in tune with each other's day-to-day business accomplishments and challenges.

For example, I feel free to give her advice, and I always read her blogs before publication—after all, she is my sister! When she wrote the following blog, I told her that I *had* to include it in this book.

The title of the blog is "Do You Need a Career Do-Over?"

If you need a career do-over, why not take a page out of Stacy London and Clinton Kelly's playbook, showcased on the TLC program *What Not to Wear*. If you have watched even a partial episode of this popular show, you have heard their dictates for female and male makeover guests. Here's my interpretation of their directives:

- Accentuate the positive.
- Change the way you look at the negatives, and make them work for you.
- Look at what you have (your current wardrobe) with a critical eye, "prune" and discard what doesn't work, and find new ways to utilize old favorites.
- Embrace your form and function; realize that you are unique.

- Approach your audience with confidence.

If you want to execute a career do-over, these are great tenets to follow. But you will also need a framework to help you through the decision-making process. During the show, the makeover guests receive the clothing rules, and then they must go shopping and make wardrobe decisions on their own.

Inevitably, the makeover guests revert to their ingrained, comfortable shopping habits—and they make purchases that do not enhance a new self-vision. After the commercial break, Stacy and Clinton come to the rescue and help the guest make better wardrobe choices. During the final minutes of the show, the makeover guests strut their stuff on a short runway and are re-introduced to their family, friends, and co-workers.

Wouldn't it be lovely if you had Stacy and Clinton to assist you in a makeover?

Unfortunately, they are busy with guests who haven't bought new clothes since the 1970s.

Now here are my tips and recommendations to further your leadership career success:

1. **Accentuate the positive.** What do you like about your current career? What's working well? Develop a strategy to capitalize on or further leverage what you have accomplished thus far.

2. **Change the way you look at the negatives, and make them work for you.** Figure out a way to tell your career story in a different manner. If you have been fired, downsized, or demoted, or have experienced any other negative work

scenarios (e.g., you sued your employer for sex or age discrimination, or you had been earning less than the market comparable), <u>focus on lessons learned and let it go</u>. You are stronger for having lived through the adversity, and actually, you are poised to widen your funnel of potential options for your life's work.

Yes, you may lack an advanced degree, a critical certification, or international experience. <u>Decide what's *really* necessary to achieve the career you want and develop a timetable to accomplish your goals.</u>

3. **Look at what you have (your current "career wardrobe") with a critical eye; "prune" and discard what doesn't work, and find new ways to utilize old favorites.** Assess the current state of your career. <u>What do you need to stop doing? What are you spending too much time on and not deriving any benefits from? Are you endlessly networking, hoping to find the right contact to offer you your next role, but you don't have the appropriate tools to enhance your reputation?</u> How might you approach finding new contacts in a more efficient manner? How can you utilize the connections of your current network to gain admittance to decision makers?

4. **Embrace your form and function; realize that you are unique.** Who you are, how you make contributions to your life's stakeholders (your spouse, your children, your family, your friends, your employer, your community), all signify your personal mission, core values, and your world impact. Recognize that your geographical

Be honest
Don't be intimidated.
Believe in yourself.
Be careful
Double check.

John Taylor
Lorraine VK, Jamie
Alana, appoint a process

Ask NATE in the knows any Jamas
Jams @ Smuls

7/10/14

sphere is larger than you envision, and free yourself and your career from artificial, self-imposed boundaries.

5. **Approach your audience with confidence.** After all is said and done, renew your confidence in yourself and your capabilities. Take the time to re-brand and re-launch your career *raison d'être* (French: "reason for existence"). When you walk the "runway" during and after your career do-over, show your value proposition in all that you do!

If you want to learn how to leverage your brand and platform, position yourself in a changing marketplace, build your marketing momentum for increased sales, or move up or transition in your career, I have just the resource for you. I invite you to review the success programs under the Global Association of High-Achieving Women at http://www.drlaureen.com/solutions/global-association-of-high-achieving-women/.

Summary Action Steps—Chapter 5

→ Going forward, do you plan to climb or leap in your career?

→ What are your brand attributes, and what is your PBS? Can you live with them?

→ Which one are you: Mentor, Mate, or Mentee? If none, why not?

→ Which of the five steps for executing a career do-over do you resonate with the most?

IS YOUR BUSINESS FABULOUS OR FAUX?

In order to be extremely successful and have a business that is fabulous and not faux, you must focus on "Taking It to a Whole **New** Level." The "Whole **New** Level" process works best when you want to out-position or out-class your competition as well as achieve business success and massive growth.

So what is the key factor to "Taking It to a Whole **New** Level"? Invest, even when it seems scary. It is very scary to invest time or money when you don't have enough of either, but you must invest time and money in yourself and your business to achieve massive success. Ask anyone who has made a major leap in their business, and you'll find that they invested a sizable amount of time or money or, in most cases, both.

Why not ask me? I have invested a large amount of time and money, and would I do it again? *Absolutely!*

The Formula

I have always been a person who loves learning new things. In 2009 I decided to focus on "Taking It to a Whole **New** Level." Obviously, I focused on the **R**e-Imagine process first. When I moved to the **R**e-Invent process, I not only invested time but

I had also invested money. I sought out preeminent business growth experts, and I invested in learning from the best.

The "Time Investment Formula" is:

$$Time \times Leverage + Power + Value = Money$$

What does it mean?

1. **Invest your <u>time</u>.** If you're agitated and over-worked, this is the mental picture you have of yourself. But what if you spent four focused hours every Monday or Tuesday just improving your business position or maximizing your platform? You would find that your feelings of agitation would diminish. You would begin to see yourself as a leader in your industry. Of course, we all know <u>perception becomes reality</u>.

   These four focused hours once a week will literally transform your business. If you don't believe me, ask the people you admire whose businesses are larger and more productive than yours. Remember, the key is always based on those adorning accessories associated with developing a "whole **new** mindset wardrobe."

   I hope you have not forgotten them. Just in case, here they are again:

Setting Intentions
Mastering Clarity
Ensuring Commitments
Practicing Consistency
Achieving Momentum

2. **Learn to <u>leverage</u> the assets you already have.** We all have books, DVDs, CDs, and programs that

we have purchased with the idea of learning more. But are you using this information? Ninety percent of you will answer "No." What was intended to be "self-help" has now become "shelf help."

My challenge to you is to leverage what you already have—you might be surprised just how valuable that CD series you purchased two years ago can be today. So gather all of your "shelf help" materials and, starting today, begin to leverage those valuable assets.

3. **Recognize the power that investing will return to you.** Money, like time, is a resource. Use this resource wisely. Here's my advice to you. Talk with people in your extended network (one or two layers up from your current group) who have made large-scale moves. Ask them what they know now that they didn't know at the beginning of their journey. Ask them to tell you the top three lessons they had to learn in order to create a power platform. Ask them to tell you their special success secret.

Model the people who are getting the results you want to have. This gives you the best chance of getting relevant information that you can apply to your business growth strategies and use to place yourself in a position of power.

Only invest when you can see a return (value or money) that makes sense for your business. Ask yourself: "Can I envision receiving a solid return on this investment in 30 days, three months, or six months?"

If you can't envision a return, then it's probably not a growth-producing investment. If you are receiving five or ten times the value of your investment, then the investment has paid for itself.

4. **Value is the biggest take-away I want you to concentrate on.** When you see coaches charging $15,000 to $20,000 for a coaching program or a coach charging $60,000 to $100,000 for a one-on-one year-long program, figure out how you can work with them. You can bet your last dollar that they are truly helping people get five, ten, fifteen, or twenty times that amount in return.

　　Here's the secret: You only invest when, in the long run, the investment will pay for itself.

> Price is what you pay. Value is what you get.
>
> —Warren Buffet

The Techniques for Becoming More Successful

When I'm coaching high-achieving women (and enlightened men), entrepreneurs, and small business owners, I am often asked, "How can I become more successful?" Well, there are multiple answers to that question.

For those of you who are women entrepreneurs or business owners, you can take note of these suggestions and apply what you feel will improve your business's success factor.

1. **Develop a plan.** You will never arrive at your destination if you start on a random path to an unknown place. You must have a *Strategic Success Plan* (re-read Chapter 4) that defines your business intentions—both short- and long-term.

2. **Identify your distractions.** If you stop at the side of the road to sightsee constantly, you will have a long delay. You may even get into unexpected trouble because you let your eyes wander from your defined course.

3. **Learn to prioritize.** Don't give too much attention to the wrong things at the wrong times. Periodically ask yourself, "How important is this?" The answer to that question will help you to stay on course.

4. **Track your progress.** Oftentimes, you have made more progress than you realize. So ask yourself: "How much have I accomplished, and how long did it take me to do that?" Be sure that your progress is reasonable for the development stage of your business, and keep moving forward.

5. **Get some help.** I am so sorry to have to tell you this, but you don't know it all. Wearing too many hats—even though hats are stylish—can be detrimental. Therefore, you need to learn from others who have accomplished the same intentions or achieved the same results that you are trying to accomplish, and apply their advice.

6. **Don't be selfish.** Some intention-oriented people have a tendency to be selfish—their frame of reference is "it's all about me." Remember that there are people around you that you can help. What goes around does come back around, so what you do for others will come back to you.

7. **Finish what you start.** If you notice that you haven't achieved your expected results, it may be because you are not finishing what you started. Learn to focus and follow through every step of the way. Be the best at everything you attempt to do before you move on to the next great idea.

Most people focus on what they are "going through"; successful people focus on what they are "going to." If you apply these techniques with focus and consistency, you will see significant progress toward your expected business results, and you will end up "getting on your dime" and "claiming your exclusive space."

> Tory Johnson, *Good Morning America*'s host of the workplace segment, says: "The goal of selling is turning 'no' into 'maybe' and 'maybe' into 'yes.' Write down your last three rejections. Did you ask why they said 'no'? If not, go back and find out. Understanding why they said 'no' helps you craft a response and maybe move you toward a 'yes.'"

What Causes a Business to Increase in Value?

Every business has the potential to be great, but the reality is that most businesses never last more than five years. Sadly, those business owners who do make it past the five-year mark earn little more than they would have made working for someone else.

In fact, if those business owners charged full price for the value of their own work and then charged for the cost of the capital they invested, only a handful would make a profit. In other words, most people are actually destroying their own wealth.

There are two reasons for this dreadful phenomenon: business owners tend to pursue a "me too" or "play a bigger game" competitive strategy, and their execution of that strategy is at best ordinary and at worst pretty appalling.

So what are the factors that increase the value of a business? They are the ones that are the "value drivers," i.e., what business appraisers consider when valuing (determining the worth of) a business. They include:

1. **Loyal clients and employees.** Turnover in clients, team, or employees can cost a business a lot of money and valuable time. Loyal clients represent recurring revenue, and loyal employees or teams can create higher levels of client satisfaction on a consistent basis.

2. **Implementation of systems.** A business is nothing more than a bundle of processes. The level to which the business is systematized will have a dramatic effect on the value of the business.

An instrument panel is the key to flying an airplane. Systems are the key to having a successful business. A business that relies on the owner being there all the time, for example, is simply valued less than a business that can run independently of the owner. The development of systems is critical to creating a business that really works and is sustainable long-term.

Without systems, you will find that you are not getting your fair share of clients, your growth is stalled, and your revenue generation is almost nonexistent!

Some examples of the systems that I recommend you implement are:

- An automatic email response program.
- Social media management.
- Consistent day-to-day business practices.
- An irresistible opt-in offer.
- Steps for up-selling your products and services.
- Strategies for building your on- and off-line platforms.

The more systems you have in place, the easier it is to grow your business and leverage your position, products, and services while achieving growth and success.

3. **A unique differentiator.** A unique differentiator is a means of distinguishing a business from its competitors. Having a differentiator means that the business may be less dependent on pricing as a strategy for business growth.

A differentiator can be the way a business packages its products or services or how it promotes itself in a way that competitors cannot match. Another differentiator could be the unique "experience" the business provides to clients. The niche that you serve is also a differentiator.

In my company, we differentiate by: "leveraging self-worth for high net-worth." We further differentiate by: "doing different things and then doing things differently." In fact, I have trademarked the doing different things slogan because I have gained many clients based on that mantra alone. Additionally, we provide clients with an experience (I call it "Putting on the Ritz"). Remember, people pay for an "experience," and I always provide my clients with what I call a "WOW Factor Experience."

4. The use of multipliers. The key is the way you use your business tools and how you use social media to spread the word about your company. You should develop multipliers that allow you to take your message from a "one-to-one" platform to a "one-to-many" platform.

Some good examples of multipliers are: newsletters, videos, radio, TV broadcasts, teleseminars, conferences, retreats, workshops, and mastermind groups. Some of the key Web-based media for using the multiplier principle are: LinkedIn, Facebook, Twitter, YouTube, and Blog Talk Radio, just to name a few.

5. The separator factor. The best way to define a separator is for you to understand the difference between a target audience and a niche.

One of the primary differences is that in most cases, when you are talking about a target audience, you already have a business started or are planning on starting one soon. You have or are currently defining your ideal clients and are determining how to promote your product or service to meet their identified needs.

With niche marketing, you are purposely building or have built a business to fit into a very specific category. Select your niche carefully, look for a definite need in the existing market, a market that is relatively undiscovered, or a market that has been overlooked by your competitors.

Another way to highlight the differences between a target audience and a niche is how much they narrow your marketplace position. An example of finding your target audience would require narrowing down the description of your typical customer, for example: "married females over age 35 with a college education."

A niche market goes beyond simply targeting someone by age, income, etc. When you develop a niche, it breaks the market into smaller segments and identifies a group of people by very specific characteristics. This is a separator.

Using the same example, you would define this target audience even more by saying that your niche is a "married female, over age 35, who is stay-at-home mom with a college education, who runs a small business from home, and who will experience tremendous business growth over the next two years."

Let's put it another way: your target market is the overall group of people you serve, and your niche is the group of people you offer your specialized products or services to because you have tailored those products or services to their specific needs.

Therefore the separator is not the target audience. You and your competitors can have the same target audience. The separator is the niche.

6. **Client focus.** A business that obtains regular, candid feedback from clients (and acts on that feedback) will generally have more loyal clients. In addition, the business that focuses on what clients really want, and what they're willing to pay for, usually has more long-term, repeat clients.

The ultra-successful business owner understands the importance of creating a "client experience," which is the first step in achieving client focus.

Utilizing these six factors can dramatically increase the profitability of a business and drive the value up substantially.

Why Brand?

Some people believe that a brand is merely a logo, a website, a catchy slogan, or company colors. Wrong, wrong, wrong. A brand is your story, your core purpose, and your client promise. Branding is your reputation; it is that core experience, that story, that uniqueness, that promise, and those core values, which are those subtle things that make you different. A brand definitely adds to any business's value.

Brand is the essence of your business. It is your company's reputation, personality, and reason for being. It's the major difference between you and your competition. It's the "mind share" you occupy in people's minds and hearts based on their cumulative experiences with you.

An effective brand directly translates into bottom line sales. If you build a brand and communicate it to the right people at the right time for the right reasons, you will attract the right clients for business growth.

Your brand forms the foundation of your overall marketing strategy, but it isn't the same thing as a marketing strategy. A brand strategy shapes your public relations message and targeted media. To make it clear, a brand is the story you tell, and public relations is the tactic (marketing strategy) for making sure that the story is heard.

Brand strategy consists of clarity, consistency, and equity.

Brand clarity attracts clients, and brand consistency makes them stick around.

When you have a brand strategy, it helps you laser-focus on activities and messages that will have the greatest impact and allows you to focus on "Taking It to a Whole **New** Level."

Lao-Tzu, a Chinese philosopher, said, "Knowing others is wisdom, knowing yourself is enlightenment." A "Zentrepreneur" is someone who risks letting go of pre-conceived notions in order to deepen their knowledge of self and beyond. But more than that, a "Zentrepreneur" is someone who has made his or her own life noble and rich beyond counting by simply living a dream defined. While an entrepreneur creates a business, a "Zentrepreneur" creates a business and a way of living life at the same time.

Exercise 6.1
Building, Positioning, and Brand Strategy

The information in this exercise will influence all of your major business decisions. It will definitely increase your chances for massive success and growth.

Below are thirteen questions to ask yourself before building your positioning and brand strategy:

1. How do you describe your company, and what you do?

2. What are your signature products, services, and pricing?

3. What are your organization's/company's strengths and weaknesses?

4. What are the adjectives and emotions around your brand?

5. Who and where is your audience, and what do you know about them?

6. What are the main benefits you provide to your clients and why can you make those claims?

7. Who are your competitors, and how are you different?

8. How do you need to communicate with current and potential clients?

9. What are your company's greatest assets and/or values?

10. Are you positioned to take advantage of these assets and/or values?

11. How has the marketplace defined your brand?

12. How do you define your brand, and is it the same as the marketplace's definition?

13. How do you measure business success?

This is an exercise that every business owner must do. So get out your pen and paper, and answer all the questions.

Once you establish your brand, you can begin to build a better relationship with prospects in order to open the door to joint ventures, promotions, and/or direct marketing initiatives. Just remember that your brand must consistently flow through the entire buying experience, or the client will abandon the buying process.

Your brand is what your customers say it is, not what you say it is. The good news is that you can shape and influence their perception by intentionally and consistently building a stand-out branded marketplace platform.

Successful business owners all have established their position in the marketplace, and they have a strategy for making their brand well known.

10 Awesome Business Tips

Here are my greatest business tips:

1. Run your life like a successful business owner (your life is the corporation, and you are the CEO).
2. Be proactive, not reactive.
3. Maximize your resources and time.
4. Leverage your brand, and develop a signature.
5. Exceed the marketplace expectations.
6. Embrace new technology, and take full advantage of social media.
7. Form collaborations and strategic alliances, build an advisory board, and garner resource partners.
8. Protect your intellectual property, trademark, and copyright as needed.
9. Build a platform that provides connections, visibility, and amplification.
10. Make it your quest to be Fit, Fine & Fabulous—not faux!

Just remember, in prosperous times build what is in your pocket. In tough times, strengthen what is in your heart.

15 Lessons I Learned from Being a CEO

I really couldn't end this chapter without sharing the lessons that I have learned in my fourteen years of being the CEO of my career, business and life. Here are the lessons that have shaped me and have helped me to master **G**rowth * achieve **S**uccess * live in strategic **A**cceleration (the GSA Factor).

One of the biggest reasons I have grown so much (especially in the last four years) is that I have followed my 3R Method: **R**e-Imagine * **R**e-Invent * **R**e-Emerge, and I've learned something from everything that I've attempted. So here's my list:

1. **Take responsibility.** You are responsible for making your future, fortune, and freedom.

2. **Learn to believe in yourself.** Nobody can tell you who you are, who you're not, what you're capable of, and what you can or cannot achieve. Only you can make your dreams come true. Only you can achieve what you've always wanted. Stop listening to people who do not have your best interests at heart. Start giving yourself permission to make this your best life *ever*.

3. **Know that you are an artist and a masterpiece**. Every one of us is a masterpiece in our own right. There is a level of genius in all of us. We are all artists who are constantly chiseling a shapeless entity to get to our own masterpiece. The design may start out shapeless, but as the artist, if you keep chiseling, the masterpiece will emerge.

   By the way, the name of my parent company is Masterpiece Solutions, LLC. Now you know why I chose that name.

4. **Resign from the role of superwoman.** As the CEO of you, realize that you deserve to be fulfilled, happy, and most importantly, healthy. That means

putting *you* first and outsourcing, delegating, and prioritizing all the rest.

5. **There is no such thing as try.** Yoda said: "Do or do not; there is no try." There is only do or do not. So many people I speak with are always talking about what they want to do, or what they could have done, or what might have been. It's time to quit waiting for permission to act and just do it (like Nike). Quit dreaming and start doing.

6. **Become accountable.** I have several accountability partners in several areas, which include my career, business and life. No man or woman is an island. Be sure to find someone who will hold you accountable to achieving your intentions. In return you may have the opportunity to do the same for them.

    This is your chance to tell someone what you're going to achieve—and their chance to kick your butt until you do!

7. **Branding is everything**. A true brand is not just a logo, slogan, or tagline. A true brand remains committed to focusing on the niche, giving target customers what they want, and staying true to the brand values. Those values last a lifetime, so make sure you establish your brand early on and then consistently apply it to everything you do, including products, design, social media profiles, websites, blogs, etc. I have learned that your brand is being tested for staying power. If you don't build it, someone else will define it—you may not like it, but the world will remember it.

8. **Get over yourself.** I have learned that as soon as you move out of your own way, you will achieve great success in business and life. My best advice is

to stop copying, competing, and comparing your-self to others and wishing you were someone else.

Stop moaning and groaning about your lack of clients, lack of money, and lack of business skills, and start taking action to learn, grow, and improve yourself on a daily basis.

The minute you take yourself out of the equa-tion and focus on providing value, helping people, and making a difference is the minute you will obtain more clients, more money, and more skills.

9. **Seek out inspiration.** Entrepreneurship can be rough. Many people go into business blindfolded because they were lured in by the thought of being their own boss with unlimited flexibility, freedom, independence, and earning.

While you will achieve all these things in time, you will also experience those moments where everything goes wrong and you can't do anything right. There will be times when you can't pay your bills, satisfy current clients, or even gain any new clients.

It is time for a wake-up call. It's time to **Re**-Imagine * **Re**-Invent * **Re**-Emerge. Go to TED.com and you will find new insight, strength, and energy.

10. **You can take time off.** Work-life balance seems to be this unachievable status that people love to talk about yet never attain. I have finally learned how to build a business around my lifestyle and have this thing called work-life balance. I got it by utilizing my creation of a Life by Design Business Model.

There was a time that I thought work, more work, and perfection were the answers, but as a seasoned Zentrepreneur and CEO, I have found that fulfillment, happiness, and purpose are what really matter. I have made sure that I enjoy life and business ownership simultaneously.

I enjoy cruising, and I attend conferences all over the world. I schedule a date with myself at least once a month (Chapter 7), and I am accomplishing those things on my Dream Big List (Chapter 7). I schedule "me" time for what I really enjoy doing every day. I am enjoying life to its fullest, and I love to laugh, even at myself.

11. **Surround yourself with genius.** Refer back to Chapter 5 (Mentor, Mate and Mentee). I have all three in my life as well as an accountability partner, resource partners, a coach, joint venture experts, and yes, collaborative relationships.

12. **Don't be cheap.** We all must watch our pennies, especially those of you who are just starting out. But as your business grows, spend money on your image, your design, brand, website, digital products, photos, your office, and a virtual assistant (a Virtual Assistant [VA] is a must). Put your money back into your business, where it counts the most, and stop being so cheap! You get what you pay for!

13. **Invest in yourself.** Spend money where it counts—on coaching, personal development, certifications, workshops, masterminds, retreats, and technology. These are the things that make running a business much easier.

14. **Leave a legacy.** This is one of the first steps to succeeding. The best possible way to build a business you love is to have a grand vision of why it's so important in the first place. A legacy means that you are doing everything for something way more important than just you (although you are very important as well). It is that mark that you want to leave on the world or that landmark of doing something that will make a difference and be remembered.

15. **Don't do it all alone**. I've talked about mentors, coaches, advisors, co-venture individuals, and resource and accountability partners in the prior lessons-learned section and in other parts of this book. When you have these individuals on your team, you have all the essential ingredients for creating a thriving company that you love and a life that you adore.

I am extremely fortunate to also have formed a couple of co-ventures with my friend and colleague, whom I will call Kate. We complement each other even though we are different in so many ways, but when we come together for business purposes, we do one thing very well—make money!

Who would have thought that two women who are very different would be so compatible in business? Now, here's my suggestion: find yourself a Kate because you can't achieve ultimate success on your own. Every business owner should have a Kate because you can't always do it alone.

Did you know that you Can Achieve Business Success by Improving YOUR "A" Game? What are you doing to ensure that you have business success? If you need help getting on your "A" Game, sign up for a complimentary 6-day e-course: http://www.highachieving-women.biz/elevations-newsletter/

Summary Action Steps—Chapter 6

What techniques have made you the most successful?

What has caused your business/company to increase in value?

Do you have a well-defined brand? If so, what is it? If not, what steps are you planning to take to define your brand?

What lessons have you learned as a CEO?

MASTERING THIS THING CALLED LIFESTYLE

This chapter will focus on lifestyle, which includes personal development and self-improvement.

So what is lifestyle? Very simply, "it is a way of life or style of living that reflects the attitudes and values of a person or group," according to freedictionary.com

My definition of *lifestyle* for the purpose of this book is: "a way of life or style of living that reflects the attitudes, values, self-growth, and the personal development of a person or group."

Self-growth and personal development include the following activities:

- developing self-awareness
- acquiring self-knowledge
- building or renewing identity
- developing strengths or talents
- identifying or improving potential
- enhancing quality of life
- fulfilling aspirations
- improving social abilities
- initiating a life enterprise or starting the process of personal autonomy

Remember, lifestyle is part of the second **"R"** of the 3R Method: **R**e-Imagine * **R**e-Invent * **R**e-Emerge. When you prepare your *Strategic Success Plan,* all of the above activities should be defined in your plan.

Right now, as of the writing of this book, I am still working on my own self-growth and personal development intentions. What is critical for me is being in a state of continuous improvement.

What Makes Self-Growth and Personal Development Critical?

Let's start with the definition of *self-growth.* It is the study and practice of improving one's life, especially career, education, relationships, health, happiness, productivity, spirituality, and other personal intentions. It is also that aspiration to realize one's higher self. It is setting the stage for the emergence of self-actualization (Maslow, 1940–1950).

The most common aspects of self-growth and personal development include establishing intentions, developing motivators, changing habits, improving awareness, and identifying one's values and beliefs.

The need for self-growth and personal development has never been more crucial than in today's marketplace. But even with all of the self-help information available today, many people are still confused on where to start.

Here are the most common principles for self-growth and personal development to help you start the process:

1. **Recognize that you are responsible for how you live your life.** People who are on the self-growth and personal development path understand that their thoughts and actions play a big role in what they achieve in life.

2. **Define what you want.** Many people go through life aimlessly, without a clear destination in mind. Ultimately, you must identify your values and intentions before you can achieve them. Then you are ready to set your GPS.

3. **Start with short-term costs—they lead to long-term benefits.** There are no magic pills, but when you have a *Strategic Success Plan*, you have a roadmap to follow. You must be willing to invest in yourself big time, which requires short-term costs but, rest assured, they will lead to long-term benefits.

4. **Know that you are always changing.** The truth is that whether you play an active role in your self-growth and personal development intentions or not, as an individual you're always changing, developing, and growing.

   We are all on some kind of self-growth and personal development path, but some people take more control over their path's destiny than others.

5. **Know that your thoughts matter.** How you think strongly influences how you act. How you act will determine the results you gain from life.

6. **Are your habits helping or hindering?** As the old saying goes, "If you keep doing what you've always done, you'll keep getting what you've always gotten."

   Sometimes you won't know what is the best course of action and what will lead to the lifestyle you desire until you have experimented with different things. Just as we should focus on changing our thoughts, we should also focus on exploring new ideas and intentions.

7. **The present moment is your place of power.** Every conscious decision you make and every action you do unfolds in the present moment. Being

more in tune with the present and more consistent will result in greater control over your day-to-day actions and growth.

8. **Learn from the past.** While you can't change your past, you can often look back on it and learn from those past mistakes and successes. When you do, you can change your future.

9. **Be optimistic about the future.** You don't know what the future may bring, but if you remain optimistic and consistent, you will act in ways that help to create the future you desire.

Self-growth and personal development is not something you learn and absorb overnight. My belief is that it is a never-ending process. Our lives are always changing, and thus there are always new and better ways for us to think and act. We learn, we apply, we grow, we invest, and we absolutely must **R**e-Invent (the second **"R"** of the 3R Method).

Self-growth and personal development means we learn to listen to our inner voice—our inner pilot. The messages of our inner voice can only be heard with a silent mind (the key word is *silent*). This inner inspiration does not come from our ego but from our soul.

Our self-growth and personal development is not just about ourselves. It is being aware of a deeper and more meaningful connection with other people. When we can extend our sense of identity, we find ourselves implementing the Golden Rule: "Do unto others as you would have them do unto you."

An overall self-growth and personal development intention is to make changes or improve certain areas of your life in which you are dissatisfied. It could also involve making changes in your behavior or attitude. For example, your self-growth and personal development intentions could be becoming a more loving person, earning more money, or developing some new skills.

For me, my intentions are based on HOPE: "Help Other People Every day."

How to Achieve Your Self-Growth and Personal Development Intentions

There are many ways you can achieve your self-growth and personal development intentions. Usually this involves gaining knowledge from books like this one.

Let's look at self-growth and personal development intentions from four different areas of your life and see how you can achieve them.

1. **Money.** If you want to improve your financial situation, you need to define the exact intentions for this aspect of your life. Maybe you want to become self-employed, be promoted, or earn more money in your business. The most important thing is to define the exact outcome that you want to experience, and then take action with consistency to achieve your financial intentions.

    It is also important to listen to your own intuition and trust your own guidance. If, however, you have limiting beliefs concerning money, your own sense of direction might hinder you. Therefore it's important to eliminate those limiting beliefs to successfully achieve your money intentions.

    Do you have a formula for eliminating limiting beliefs? If not, here's one you can try:

    1. List your limiting beliefs concerning money.
    2. Where do these limiting beliefs come from?
    3. How have these limiting beliefs impacted your wealth?
    4. What will you do to diminish your limiting beliefs?

2. **Health.** If your intention is to improve your health, you should be specific concerning the improvements you would like to make.

    What are the exact areas to be improved? Be sure they are clearly defined and written. Develop a plan and conduct research on how to heal your condition or improve your health. It might mean seeking a second opinion, starting an exercise program, taking all-natural supplements, getting more sleep, etc.

3. **Mind.** Your self-growth and personal development intentions might be how to gain peace of mind, gain more awareness, or improve your perception or instincts. These objectives center on more "mind power," which gives you a sense of empowerment and a sense of your own self-worth.

    The basis for gaining "mind power" is to understand that you create your own reality. If you still believe that you are a victim of random circumstances, then you don't understand that your thoughts govern your reality. Only when you fully understand the concept of conscious creation will you be able to make changes and improve your life.

4. **Growth.** Always seek to continue the learning process. Secure the best possible education. At a minimum, in today's marketplace, a bachelor's degree is mandatory.

    Also obtain certifications and/or professional licenses to remain current in your career or business and learn something new everyday.

As you can see, self-growth and personal development is not just one single target. Your self-growth and personal development intentions can be related to any area of your life or any aspect of it that requires improvement.

Success in any area of your life is not made from the "home runs." Success is made from the little things that you do consistently everyday to build a successful outcome.

The 10.5 Best Tips for Self-Improvement

1. **Wake up early.** The early bird does not get the worm; the early bird makes the money. He/she is working while others are sleeping.

2. **Love what you do.** If you don't love it, you will never rise to the top. Love it, or leave it.

3. **Focus on life-long efforts.** Dedicate yourself to being a life-long student. How many books did you read last year?

   Recently, I was speaking with an executive coach, and she told me that she read 50 books last year. I read 20 books last year. Both of our totals do not include e-books, white papers, or articles. How many books have you read?

4. **Convert anger to resolve.** Anger is the biggest waste of energy on the planet. It blocks positive thoughts, creative thoughts, and self-growth.

5. **Convert barriers to breakthroughs.** You may think of barriers as objections or even rejections. Stick with it until you win, and you will gain personal and mental dominance.

6. **Accept every "no" as a "not yet."** You don't hear with your ears. You hear with your mind. The way you accept other people's words will determine your fate. Gain an attitude of positive acceptance.

7. **Watch little or no television.** You'll never succeed watching television. Convert TV time to study time. Convert TV time to preparation time. Convert TV time to thinking time. Invest your time—don't spend it.

Did you know that the average person at age 65 has watched nine years of television? What a waste of time.

8. **Read for twenty minutes every morning.** Reading provides the opportunity for quiet insight. You can reflect on the ideas and thoughts of others and immediately convert them to your own success formula. Your best chance for success is reading. You learn to earn, but you read to succeed.

9. **Write for twenty minutes every morning.** What should you write about? Anything you want! Begin to clarify your thoughts and ideas in writing.

10. **Call the people you love**. Tell your loved ones that you love them. Love is not motivation. Love is inspiration. To be your best, you must go beyond motivation to inspiration.

10.5. **Tell yourself you are the best.** "I am the greatest of all time." Muhammad Ali said that thousands of times. Millions of people agreed that he was the greatest of all time. He began that journey by telling himself first. So can you!

Pursing your dreams requires you to leave your established comfort zone and to push into areas where at first you may feel that you have less control. That means pushing beyond what is known to you, taking risks and learning to view failure as merely a step, rather than a defeat.

—Steadman Graham

What about Lifestyle?

Lifestyle is a term to describe the way a person lives, which was originally coined by Austrian psychologist Alfred Adler in 1929. I believe that improving your lifestyle also requires that you identify what you can do to establish more meaning and purpose. You will become conscious of what is happening within and around you.

As you develop your *Strategic Success Plan,* your current lifestyle and expected lifestyle will be key as your plan unfolds. Be sure to sharpen your interest in learning, knowing, feeling, thinking, and acting. Learn more about who you are through reflection. Develop a sense of adventure and a desire to know more.

Allow yourself the opportunity to become involved in activities that give you a sense of self-worth and joy. Find satisfaction from the things you do that stretch you to experience the best.

Lifestyle fit is the process of knowing people from different backgrounds and cultures. When you master the art of knowing others, you will know more about yourself, and your mind will open to new concepts that will help you understand and appreciate life and living.

Practice making good choices and decisions. Place yourself in a state of mind that allows you to function at your best. Learn how to truly take control of your personal, professional, and social life. Always use your time in the best possible way.

1. **Focus on your current moment.** Be happy with yourself in the present moment, but continue to design a better future. The front windshield of life is much larger than your rear view mirror. Start the process of creating and fashioning your life by design. Stay positive so that you will notice God's blessings in your life.

   Live by your personal mission statement and core values. Dictate your own destination, and choose to create your own happiness. Maintain a Fit, Fine & Fabulous balance in your relationships, career, business and life so that you will feel in control.

2. **Perform generous acts.** Practice the act of giving. Listen to what others have to say. Always speak kind and encouraging words. Always offer a smile. Give love, support, and warmth. Speak the truth and live an integrity-based life. Give your time and energy to bring joy to others.

Give thanks and learn to be grateful daily. See the beauty and positive intentions in others. Send out positive thoughts and energy daily.

3. **Practice healthy living.** The most vital aspect of living is being in good health. Many people who have everything but aren't healthy feel that life is not worth living. Healthy living consists of eating well, regular exercise, proper breathing, being in healthy relationships, enjoying a loving life without greed, jealousy, and resentments, and, of course, without addictions to toxic substances.

4. **Manage your emotions.** You can control how you feel. You can respond to adversity without breaking down or giving up. Let your emotions trigger you to have more love and a higher standard of living. Practice remaining calm and composed in difficult situations. Add a sense of humor to your setbacks. Don't bring your anger into another day. Settle it before you slumber. If you are feeling lost and out of control, it's time to touch base with your inner Fit, Fine & Fabulous.

Put aside a little quiet time each day to gather your thoughts, recognize the emotions that are blocking your progress, and give thanks for the emotions that are supporting you during your transition.

5. **Make progress each day.** Being lifestyle fit should be part of your *Strategic Success Plan.* Develop a list of your intentions. Do something every day without fail, and keep going until you achieve each of the intentions defined in your *Strategic Success Plan.*

I have found that the key to achieving a Fit, Fine & Fabulous lifestyle is to be self-disciplined—above all, consistent—and to make sure that your career, business and life evolve around your personal core values.

Personal Core Values

Along life's journey, I have developed five personal core values. They represent the things I want to have in my life. I always revisit these core values as I establish new intentions.

- **Love.** It is the central theme in my life. I want and need love, and I have a lot of love to give. Love for life, for people, for nature, for the things I do, and so on. But most important is my love for God, family, and friends.
- **Fun.** I love laughing, and I love to do fun things, with other people or alone. Time is too precious not to have fun, but it's so easy to let this one slip away. Sometimes we're just too serious, and it's so easy to get caught in that atmosphere of "seriousness."
- **Freedom.** It is a core value that's really important to me. I place significance on all facets of life, from the physical freedom of movement to the mental freedom of thought and decisions and everything between.
- **Authenticity.** It is the things I do, the things that connect to who I am. Knowing my standards and

having a clear direction in my life are part of my authenticity.

- **Growth.** It is so critical. I'm fascinated by intentions and potential. I love the energy and creativity associated with fulfilling intentions for myself and helping others to achieve remarkable growth.

Your personal core values may differ from mine, and that's okay—just make sure that you know your personal core values.

Becoming lifestyle fit will move you from good to great, from ordinary to extraordinary, and from just performing well to stellar performance. Lifestyle fit is the act of going from good to better to best in all areas of your life based on your personal core values.

Exercise 7.1
It's Time to Start Dating

Here is what I would like for you to do. Make a date with yourself at least once a month. Be sure to put the date on your calendar. You must devote the entire day to just you. I want you to plan it as you would any other date with a colleague, peer, family member, or friend. Be sure to pick a venue, make a reservation, and budget for the experience.

Okay, in case you have never dated yourself and you are wondering what to do—here are a few date examples:

- Pack a lunch and go for a hike.
- Attend a day-long conference.
- Check into an upscale hotel (one with all of the amenities—I am a Ritz Carlton girl) and pamper

yourself the entire weekend (this is a great time to know yourself again).

- What about spending the day on the golf course? I am a former member of Women on Course (it's a great organization). I still have not mastered golf.
- Take a dance lesson, have lunch (some place that is exotic and unusual), and go shopping.
- Attend a ballet or the opera (I love *Madame Butterfly* and *Miss Saigon*).
- Take off your shoes, roll up your pants, and walk along the beach.

Two Fridays ago, I took a friend to lunch. Okay, I must admit, before lunch I took a long, hot bubble bath—it was the best. After lunch, we went shopping at my favorite boutique (I found some great designer bargains). At the end of the day, I had a well-deserved body massage, and I curled up in bed and watched one of my favorite movies (*The Devil Wears Prada*).

Please let me know how you enjoyed your date with yourself!

The biggest adventure you can take is to live
the life of your dreams.

—Oprah Winfrey

Dream Big

Part of the 3R Method: **R**e-Imagine * **R**e-Invent * **R**e-Emerge is to always think big and focus on "Taking It to a Whole **New** Level." What has helped me think big is doing unusual things.

Why not make a Dream Big List of 20 or 30 things you would like to accomplish in your lifetime that you haven't accomplished yet. Some of the things on this list should be a bit unrealistic (out-of-the-ordinary and unusual) for you.

I have learned that the secret to a happy life is to have someone to love, something to do, and something to look forward to. Here is part of my Dream Big List:

- Learn to box (I have already purchased pink boxing gloves).
- Purchase a baby grand piano and take piano lessons.
- Start a foundation for a worthy cause (for me, homeless women with children).
- Hike and climb Machu Picchu.
- Write a book. (Oh wow—this is done!)
- Travel to a different country once a year (so far I have been to Switzerland, Spain, Italy, France and Bermuda; next year I am going to Belize, Australia, and New Zealand).
- Learn to kayak.
- Take a helicopter ride.
- Participate in walk-a-thons for worthy causes.
- Climb a rock wall (now that is going to take some getting into shape).

Pick one thing from your list each year and take action toward creating your big dream.

Even though you may have scars and your life may not have been the best, know that if you keep going, your scars will become stars. You simply must put the passion back into your life—Dream Big!

You can't control the length of your life—but you
can control its width and depth.

You can't control the contour of your face—but you
can control its expression.

You can't control the weather—but you can control
the atmosphere of your mind.

—Anonymous

Now that we have mastered lifestyle, it's logical to look at relationships.

Would you like to find out How to "Show Off" Your Credibility Factor for *Revenue Acceleration!* Credibility is just as important as the know, like, trust, and value factors. Visit www.drlaureen.com.

Summary Action Steps—Chapter 7

→ What limiting beliefs do you need to eliminate in order to move forward?

→ What one thing can you improve now that will have a dramatic impact? Lose weight 7/15

→ Are you living a life by design? If yes, can you make it better? How? If no, what can you do now to get started?

BUILT TO LAST—
POSITIVE RELATIONSHIPS

In the previous chapter, I discussed lifestyle. Without relationships, lifestyle would have little meaning or significance.

I have found that most people have an idea of what constitutes the quality of a good or appropriate relationship.

We cause ourselves needless stress by comparing our own career's, business's, or life's relationships with the idea of what a relationship should be, then concluding that ours are defective by comparison or great by elimination.

The definition of *relationship* is "a connection, association, or involvement," according to freedictionary.com.

If you look back at Chapter 3, you can revisit The Wheel of Life. Note that relationships are one of the segments on The Wheel of Life.

As an extrovert, people's interactions are very important to me. Even if you are an introvert, relationships, friends, and family are the keys to your career, business and life successes.

Relationships come in a variety of shapes and sizes: never-ending relationships, survival relationships, career relationships, validation relationships, business relationships, healing relationships, life relationships, transitional relationships, and the list goes on and on. In this chapter, I will discuss family, career, and business relationships.

But the most exciting, challenging and significant
relationship of all is the one you have with yourself.
And if you can find someone to love the you that
you love, well, that's fabulous.

Building Family Relationships

I believe that the most important relationship that anyone
can have is the family relationship, which is second only to a
relationship with God. When you have positive family relationships, it also colors your career and business relationships.
Here are four ways to build positive family relationships:

1. **As often as possible, eat dinner together as
   a family and not in front of the TV.** Eating as
   a family is a healthy habit that helps to bring everyone closer. Research (Parents.com) indicates that
   eating together teaches children proper etiquette
   and also encourages them to eat healthier foods.

   Even if you don't have children, eating with
   your family allows you to relax from the busy pace
   of work and the opportunity to discuss your day's
   activities.

2. **Spend recreational time with family, doing
   activities that all members enjoy.** For example, you can play board or online games, bake
   cookies, play softball, or read a book together.

   Information from the University of Delaware's
   Cooperative Extension emphasizes that even
   though it can be challenging to make time for
   family members, creating regular family rituals,
   such as fun events, can help you reconnect each
   week so you know each other better.

3. **Respect each other's personal space.** If your husband asks for some alone time, give it to him. Don't snoop through your teenagers' things when they aren't around (unless there is a very good reason). Everyone requires some time alone, and respecting privacy is one of the things that build solid relationships.

   If you have several children, it's very important to give each one of them time alone with you. Take your son to a sporting event while your spouse takes your daughter to a movie. Did you know that alone time with parents helps children feel special and more grounded?

4. **Allow everyone in the family to openly communicate his/her feelings.** In order to maintain healthy family relationships, each member must be able to communicate freely with one another as well as listen effectively.

   Listening allows you to learn more about your family members' thoughts and beliefs; communication allows you to express yourself and share happiness, and it relieves frustration and other emotions.

   It is important that you do not interrupt a family member. Instead, listen until he/she is finished, and then relate how you feel. This effective type of two-way communication can prevent and solve arguments, and it goes a long way in keeping family relationships healthy.

Building Career Relationships

One of the most important career management habits that you can develop for career success and resiliency is paying regular attention to building career relationships. Remember that mentors, role models, and coaches can help you connect, gain support, develop, and excel in your career—but you must work at the relationships consistently.

There are numerous ways to build career relationships. Here are some examples:

- Observe colleagues and your boss in meetings or other work interactions. Figure out what they do well and what you can learn by watching them or talking with them about their processes.
- Share your career intentions with your supervisor and colleagues. Your supervisor will better understand your desire to work on various projects if you share your reasoning and needs for self-development.
- Ask friends, colleagues (former and current), supervisors (former and current), professional contacts, career mentors, and coaches for feedback on your strengths, weaknesses, and areas that need growth.
- Know yourself and your intentions, and learn how to articulate this information clearly and with enthusiasm.
- Learn to listen to others and discover their intentions and skills. Periodically send information that may be of interest to them.
- Respond to others when asked for feedback, consultation, or collaboration, and be generous with reciprocating your time.
- Figure out what relationships you want to develop, what relationships you already have, and how to reach and stay in touch with them.
- Update people in your network periodically on your career development endeavors.

- Don't expect any one person to play every possible function in your career development, whether it's your supervisor, your spouse, or your partner. Diversify your network.
- Thank people for their time, feedback, and help.

When I worked in corporate America before starting Dr. Laureen International, I was always on the lookout for the go-to people when I started a new job. I focused on the people who knew how to get things done, no matter where they fit on the organizational chart.

One of the best ways to find the go-to people is to ask the following leading question after meeting any new person: "Who do you recommend I speak to and get to know?" You'll know you've discovered a go-to person when several employees provide the same name and they say, "Oh, you must meet so-and-so!"

Now that you've identified the go-to people, go to them. Begin cultivating relationships with these go-to people. Make sure you understand the structure of the division in which a go-to person works and schedule "get-to-know-you" meetings. This will allow you to develop a relationship with them and do a little bit of promoting of your talents and interests.

Finally, have an early conversation with your manager that involves the development of your 30/60/90-Day Plan. This plan should clearly state what you intend to accomplish in your first three months. While this is a common best practice, you can show your manager and colleagues your focus on collaboration and your ability and willingness to tap into others' expertise by incorporating ideas and suggestions (with appropriate credit) from the meetings you set up during your first days and months on the job.

Perhaps the most important piece of advice for your first 90 days is to establish yourself as a team player by doing more listening than speaking. Too many new employees fall into the trap of trying to prove their worth by offering unsolicited opinions or making odious comparisons to "how we did it at my last job."

You are in a new position, and your employer and fellow employees want to know you are on their team now and that you are 100 percent committed. The best way to prove your worth is to be a focused listener to your teammates.

Building Business Relationships

It's no secret that we do business with people we know, like, and trust. Getting to this point in a business relationship doesn't happen overnight. Commit to consistency, give unconditionally, and before you know it, your collection of business cards will turn into something tangible—lifelong partnerships that can stand the test of time.

Consistently show sincere interest in other people and devote time to following up and knowing them better. Here are three tips to help you start in the right direction:

- Ask the right questions. This is the best way to start a conversation. Be sure to ask meaningful and relevant questions. Think about it—do you really want to know what the other person thinks about the weather, or would you rather find out the latest book they've read or movie they've seen? These types of questions provide insight into someone's personality, which leads to finding out more about his or her likes and dislikes. By all means, avoid the most boring question: "So what do you do?"
- Become a better listener. It's pointless to ask the right questions if you're not listening to what's being said. Always be present and focus on what's taking place right now in front of you. Not only

do you have to be aware of what's being said, but you also must sharpen your skills so that you can identify what's not being said.

- Master the follow-up game. If you've been sending those cookie-cutter emails thanking people for their time, you're totally blowing the follow-up opportunity. Seriously, in the past, I've made the same mistake, so you're not alone.

  Don't run yourself ragged trying to immediately connect a person—right there on the spot—with someone you think they should know. The best time to do this is in your follow-up note. Why? It lets them know you were thinking of them after you met, you actually spent some time reflecting on what they said, and then you took the time to carefully recommend specific people and resources. Surprise them by not sending an email; instead, give them a phone call. Yes, phones still work for calling. Be personable, memorable, and helpful, and it doesn't hurt to add a bit of humor to the mix.

We've all heard that it's not what you know but whom you know (or better yet, who knows you) that determines your success. Who do you think is glad that they know you?

When you offer value to another person, then they have a reason to want to stay connected with you. Here are five tips that allow for long-term solid business relationships:

- Approach each contact as if it is the beginning of a long-term, high-value relationship. Expect great things over the long term, and do your part to help both of you achieve your desired outcomes.
- Make a plan to be loyal to your connections and customers, whether they are loyal to you or not.

Always be trustworthy, so they will want to be loyal in return.

- Continually ask yourself: "What else can I do for them without asking for something in return?"
- Give them the option to occasionally "have a bad hair day" without becoming upset or judgmental. No one is always at his or her best.
- Don't always ask for something at every encounter. Occasionally just give something or just listen to them without trying to "fix" them or sell to them.

If you don't put enough effort into nurturing your business relationships, they will wither away.

There are three ways to destroy a business relationship, and there are also three ways to nurture a relationship.

Destroy a Business Relationship	Nurture a Business Relationship
1. Criticism	1. Appreciation
2. Blame	2. Affection (Acknowledgement)
3. Neglect	3. Attention

Are you destroying or nurturing?

Summary Action Steps—Chapter 8

How can you improve your family relationships?

How can you improve your career relationships?

How can you create better business relationships?

HAVING IT ALL—BEING MENTALLY AND PHYSICALLY FIT

Being mentally fit means having a sharp memory, a creative mind, a positive attitude, and an optimistic outlook on life. It is that healthy state of mind that allows you to resist hopelessness, negativity, blame, despair, resentment, worry, ungratefulness, and anxiety.

The phrase "mental health and fitness" means something different to everyone. Being mentally fit goes hand-in-hand with having a fit body; living and working in a satisfying, stimulating, and nurturing environment; continual personal and social development; and achieving spiritual fulfillment.

The mind and body do not function independently; rather, they are intimately linked, and the health of one is dependent on the health of the other.

A major ingredient for a lifetime of mental fitness is a healthy attitude. Maintaining a healthy attitude requires daily exercise, utilization of stress management techniques, and the practice of mental gymnastics.

A good attitude is a valuable ingredient for quality of life. A healthy mental attitude is a positive outlook on life, where there is an abundance of love, hope, graciousness, peace, joy, and gratefulness. These emotions greatly enhance our inner being and our outward appearance.

The Building Blocks for a Healthy Attitude

When you strive to fill your mind with uplifting thoughts and your days with feel-good activities, there is little room for negativity. Your level of joy and quality of life will improve. Here is what works for me:

1. **Have purpose.** A strong sense of purpose in life is a must if you are going to maintain a positive attitude. You are on this earth for a reason. Discover your passion and pursue it. Make your dream your work, and work your dream. Your purpose is all the information that you uncovered in your W5 Portfolio (Chapter 2).

2. **Strive for excellence.** When you give your best on a daily basis, you will feel good about who you are. If you compromise your standards, you undermine your self-esteem.

3. **Begin every day with affirmations.** Repeat each of the following sentences three times while standing in front of a mirror. Say them with authority:

   "I will have a fantastic day."
   "I consider today a blessing."
   "I am better and wiser today than yesterday."

4. **Exercise daily.** Daily exercise has a positive effect on negative stressors. Exercise, like laughter, produces relaxing, mood-enhancing endorphins that help you to better deal with whatever comes your way. Some form of physical exercise is mandatory to becoming Fit, Fine & Fabulous.

Stepping Stones for a Healthy Life

Here are 10 tips that have helped me on the road to being Fit, Fine & Fabulous. They have become my stepping stones for being my best.

1. Expect to fail a number of times before you achieve success.
2. Learn to trust your instincts, and don't judge or ignore your moods.
3. Remember, as long as you stay open-minded, it does not hurt to try new things.
4. Stay focused on what success means to you, not what it means to others.
5. Know that you are unique, but learn from what you see others do.
6. Do not set intentions (goals) that you are not likely to achieve.
7. Celebrate every success before you start the next success.
8. Look for the right health and wellness solutions that work for you.
9. Stop criticizing your looks, your body, and who you are.
10. Know that you will fall off the horse from time to time; just be prepared to keep climbing back on.

Your Environment Equals Your Mood

The connection between your home, work, and family environments and the state of your mind is a widely accepted way to achieve success. Some believe that when all are in alignment, happiness and much success follows.

Many people practice the ancient Chinese science and art of *Feng Shui* (a 3,000-year-old environmental philosophy) as a practical way to improve many aspects of life while balancing their environment.

David Daniel Kennedy, in his book *Feng Shui Tips for a Better Life,* says, "*Feng Shui* is the art of using arrangement and placement to improve your life. It is a way of manipulating environmental factors to enhance the life energy of the environmental factors and improve your destiny. Life energy, known as *chi* to the Chinese, is the basic force that animates all living things. Your own flow of *chi* will improve and strengthen as you apply *Feng Shui* principles to your life."

Your physical surroundings definitely have a significant impact on your mood. The next time you enter a cluttered room, whether it's in your home or your office, take note of any physical sensations you experience. A room filled with too much stuff—too many objects, even if they are valuable objects—occupies too much of your "calming space" and can result in internal chaos.

I once heard that your home and workspaces mirror your internal condition—that your surroundings are a reflection of the emotional peace or turmoil you are currently experiencing in your life. I agree with this statement. Your visual stimuli, whether good or bad, has a powerful impact on your mood.

Below are some suggestions for improving positive energy flow, both internally and externally, and for instilling harmony in your daily life:

1. **Use simple, functional, aesthetically pleasing furnishings.** Too much of a good thing makes your rooms appear smaller and less warm. A room that appears crowded may simply need some tidying up or furniture rearrangement in order to provide a sense of expansiveness.
2. **Organize.** Remove the stacks of magazines and piles of junk mail that you've been meaning to get rid of but haven't. Organize and file important items, and toss out the rest.

3. **Don't procrastinate.** Either get the job done, or just say no! Prioritize your daily schedule and keep it updated in one central place using today's technology (smart phone, iPad, iPhone, or digital calendar).
4. **Tidy up.** Keep every room in your home or office as clean as possible. Dirt is distracting and unhealthy.
5. **Live and work in a well-lit place.** Lights lift your mood and make all rooms appear larger and brighter.
6. **Live with plants.** Plants are peace-givers. Place natural plants in all your surroundings to freshen the air, relax the eyes, and soothe a busy mind. If your budget is tight and you've only got a few pieces of furniture to fill a room, plants make a perfect, inexpensive furniture replacement.

Stay Mentally Sharp for Life

"Use-dependent plasticity" is the neurological phrase for the idea of "use it or lose it." Scientists have long speculated that we are using only 10 percent of our brain capacity, leaving 90 percent potentially untapped. What if you could access, cultivate, or unleash this vast creative energy? How different would you be?

In the daily practice of exercising your brain past its current limits, attempting to reach beyond the obvious solutions to a problem will create new and permanent neutral pathways in the brain. Exercising the brain is believed to stimulate peak functioning. As you age, it is important to keep your mind active and not become a mental couch potato. Remaining mentally sharp is one of the keys to aging well and remaining forever young.

Recently I read a quote by Lucille Ball that stated the secret to staying young is: "to live honestly, eat slowly, and lie about your age."

In order to forge ahead into uncharted mental territory and expand your thought processes, you need to stimulate, challenge, and stretch your mind daily to keep it resilient, creative, and flexible. By challenging your brain to create new neural pathways, you begin to open the untapped 90 percent of your brain. This will help keep your memory and intelligence functioning at high levels.

Mental Gymnastics

Many of us grew up attending schools where the educational agenda was primarily to target the left side of the brain by requiring logical and rational studies that used structured, sequential thought. Subjects such as reading, writing, mathematics, spelling, foreign language studies, and other structured, sequential thoughts all engage the left side of your brain.

The right side of the brain is what many consider to be the "artsy" side. To stimulate this more creative part of your mind, become involved with the arts, sports, and music. Remember, right-brain learning nurtures the development of intuition and the ability to facilitate insight. For me, I have found music to be quite stimulating.

The best mental workouts involve stimulating the right and left sides of your brain. To accelerate your thinking, try doing things with the opposite hand. Write, dial the phone, brush your hair and teeth, apply your moisturizer, use a calculator, or move the computer mouse with your "lazy" hand. This teaches the non-dominant side of your brain to develop coordination.

Challenge your brain by taking a break from your routine. Drive a different route to work, take the kids to school instead of sending them out to the bus, wake up an hour earlier and then meditate or take a walk, or even rearrange your normal daily or weekly activities.

The key to keeping the brain healthy for a lifetime is to exercise it on a daily basis. It's just like any other muscle—it must be worked out in order to stay fit and functional.

So for those of you who work out physically—don't forget to work out mentally.

We all must be willing to take action to move towards the limits of what's possible and to finally realize that everything is possible.

How to be Physically Fit

I can't imagine my life without exercise. Even though I have some major health challenges, it's still mandatory that I exercise to remain physically fit and mentally alert. I truly believe that being physically fit has, in fact, increased my life span and has allowed me to do some things that otherwise I would not have been able to accomplish with my health challenge.

I work out three times a week for a little over an hour each time. I try to achieve a bonus workout once a week on either Saturday or Sunday. Lately, I have skipped Saturday and Sunday; I prefer having fun. If I don't do the bonus workout, I don't beat myself up—I just continue to enjoy life.

Willie E., my personal trainer, is awesome. He has pushed me to achievements that I did not realize I could accomplish. To date, I have lost 55 pounds, not to mention numerous inches. My body, needless to say, is Fit, Fine & Fabulous.

His favorite saying is "Nothing tastes as good as thin feels."

Creative Solutions for Your Exercise Excuses

Make this year a year of movement. It's important that you not only exercise your business muscles and your career muscles, but also your physical muscles.

I read a great article by Taisha Hayes (featured expert on

Dr. Oz) who, at age 23, weighed nearly 300 pounds. Realizing she needed to make a change, Taisha lost 130 pounds without giving up her appreciation for food.

In the process of losing weight, she learned to love exercise and became a personal trainer. Here are some of her recommendations:

1. Prepare exercise clothes the night before, and keep your bag by the door or in your car every day for easy access.

2. Exercise during commercial breaks while watching TV.

3. Exercise on the floor while supervising your children at play or while they are completing their homework. You can perform squats, lunges, and sit-ups while providing a positive example of how important it is to make exercise a priority.

4. Exercise while waiting for the microwave to ding. Perform squats or sit-ups and see how many you can complete before your food is ready. You will be shocked at how much you can strengthen and challenge your muscles in a few short minutes.

5. Exercise while waiting for the train or bus to arrive. Squats, stretches, or rhythmic tightening of your abs or gluts are a great way to pass the wait time, and they will keep you warm in cold weather.

6. Exercise during your lunch hour. Spend 15–30 minutes of your lunchtime walking up and down the stairs of your office building.

7. Exercise while you read/study. Do the "hold the plank" exercise or a wall squat as you read. See how long you can hold the squat position (i.e., how many words, paragraphs or pages can you read before you must stop and rest). Plus, exercise increases energy and will help keep you alert during long study sessions.

8. Practice the 10-Minute Rule: complete at least 10

minutes of physical activity each day. Every little bit counts and it is a great way to form the exercise habit. Would you believe that I do butt tucks while waiting in line at the grocery store?

9. Remember there is absolutely nothing selfish when you make your health and fitness a priority. You must take care of yourself to be able to help anyone else.

Once you make scheduling daily exercise a priority, you will be amazed at how many routines you can create to exercise your physical muscles.

10.5 Things You Can Do Today to Feel Fabulous

Below is a list of my recommendations for feeling fabulous.

1. Drink lots of water (I am drinking 48–64 ounces a day—it took a while for me to reach this point).
2. Send a personal note to someone.
3. Try one new fruit or vegetable (I am going to try eggplant—hope it tastes good).
4. Add a favorite aroma to your surroundings. (I like Frutopia scented soy candles.)
5. Take a brisk walk, and hug a tree along the way— yes, hug a big tree!
6. Think positive, smile, and laugh out loud.
7. Eat a healthy lunch; enjoy a protein drink or smoothie.
8. Take a 20-minute power nap.
9. Plan something that you can look forward to accomplishing (a date with yourself).
10. Volunteer at a homeless shelter, food pantry, or children's facility (it can be just one hour). I promise, it will change your life.
10.5. Treat yourself to a great pair of shoes.

To me, this is one of the most important chapters under the **R**e-Invent process. Without good health, nothing else matters. If you are not in the best of health now, start slowly working toward achieving good health.

Without going into all of the details concerning my health challenges, I can tell you that if you start slow and remain consistent, you will achieve the momentum you need to do more. There was a time in my life when I could only perform on the elliptical machine for one minute and twenty-three seconds. At that most health-challenged time, that one minute and twenty-three seconds was equivalent to someone with excellent health completing one hour on the elliptical. It took everything that I had to complete that one minute and twenty-three seconds.

The point is, I kept trying, and I increased my time on the elliptical machine until I reached 20 minutes, which, for me, was nothing short of remarkable.

Remember those adorning accessories you learned about in Chapter 3:

Setting Intentions

Mastering Clarity

Ensuring Commitments

Practicing Consistency

Achieving Momentum

They are the keys to being mentally and physically fit. Now that you are on the path to being mentally and physically fit, I'll turn my attention to spiritual fitness in the next chapter.

The true indicator of a life well lived is not about what you are doing or where you are going; it is about how far you've come from yesterday to today!

–Jon Satin and Chris Pattay

Summary Action Steps—Chapter 9

→ What are you doing to stay physically fit?

→ What are you doing to stay mentally fit?

→ What three things make you feel fabulous?

GETTING IN TOUCH WITH YOUR SPIRITUAL SELF

Today there is a lot of talk concerning the mind/body/spirit connection. What does this mean to you? Have you ever considered how fit you are spiritually? Have you ever thought of it in these terms? Consider for a moment that spiritual fitness leads to emotional and physical well-being as a natural consequence.

Obviously, when we experience peace in our lives, we are healthier, happier, and more creative. But how do we reach that point? What do we have to do to achieve this? And when we do achieve it, how long does it last?

When you are spiritually fit, you have freed-up energy. You have more mental energy, you feel lighter, your mood isn't uneven, and your memory sharpens dramatically. You are easier to love, be around, and, in some cases, tolerate. People will actually enjoy being around you, and you will actually feel like being around others.

Getting Started

How do you start? Very simple:

- Focus on who you are and your gifts and talents.
- Resist strong pressure from family and friends.

- Practice optimism.
- Disregard any self-imposed limits that may prevent you from growth, fulfillment, and achievement.
- Eliminate anything that you are tolerating.
- Do away with those things that drain your energy.
- Stop putting up with what's dragging you down.
- Continuously smile (when you smile, the whole world smiles with you).
- Accept who you are. Know that you are a valuable jewel.

When you define your career, business, life, and spiritual intentions in your *Strategic Success Plan,* it makes them real. By clearly identifying what you want, both your conscious and subconscious mind will adjust your thinking process and align with your spiritual side.

> There's no such thing as an obstacle, only the opportunity to create. That obstacle is now asking you to evolve!

Finding Your Spiritual Side

I recently read an article by Nicole Yorio, a freelance writer and editor for Redbook, entitled "Find Your Spiritual Side." I resonated with what Nicole was saying, and below is an excerpt of the article "Find Your Spiritual Side."

1. **Look within.** Whether you choose an organized religion or a more individual practice, the spiritual journey is a personal one. To begin, search within and ask, *What do I want out of life? Why am I here? What is my purpose?* Reflect on what spirituality means to you and what role you want it to

play in your life, and you'll have a better sense of how to embark on your own path.

2. **Be present.** Instead of dwelling on the past or worrying about the future, slow down, tap into your feelings as they unfold, and find the beauty in the now.

3. **Let go**. Put faith in the unknown, and give up trying to control how your life will play out. When you embrace your spiritual side, you're choosing to believe that God, the universe, or the divine has your best interest in mind.

4. **Meditate.** It involves turning off your mind so you can connect with your spirit and your own peaceful center.

   It can be as simple as adding a one-minute pause to your day or taking a few deep breaths to create an oasis of calm in your world. That moment of quiet helps you free yourself to find insights that are typically drowned out by the noise of everyday life.

5. **Stay connected.** Living spiritually is a daily choice, which requires more than going to a weekly religious service. You need to stay in touch with your own spirituality and spend time with people on a similar path. Surround yourself with visual cues such as short prayers or pictures that remind you of the person you want to be.

Acknowledge the Facts

For me, I acknowledge the fact that I am a spirit with a physical body, not a physical body with a spirit. I have developed the happiness habit by always looking at the bright side of life and endeavoring to be happy in all my quests.

I have learned that happiness must come from within, and I don't let any circumstance decide my happiness or my fate. I have learned how to be tolerant, patient, tactful, and considerate toward others. I read spiritual and uplifting books, and I meditate for at least 10 minutes every day.

This is my Fit, Fine & Fabulous spiritual motto:

Always take a deep breath and then let it go...
Be thankful for <u>this</u> moment...
It is the only one I know that I have for sure.

Take Time

Here are eleven very important things we all should do each and every day. You will feel happy and whole when you take the time to do each of them.

Take Time to Think: A Poem of Encouragement

Take time to think:
it is the source of power.

Take time to read;
it is the foundation of wisdom.

Take time to play;
it is the secret of staying young.

Take time to be quiet;
it is the opportunity to see God.

Take time to be aware;
it is the opportunity to help others.

Take time to love and be loved;
it is God's greatest gift.

Take time to laugh;
it is the music of the soul.

Take time to be friendly;
it is the road to happiness.

Take time to dream;
it is what the future is made of.

Take time to pray;
it is the greatest power on earth.

Take time to give;
it is too short a day to be selfish.

—Anonymous

Don't forget to take the time to do each one of these!

There is no better way to energize your body, mind, and spirit than by taking good care of yourself and by taking time for yourself.

You will find renewed happiness when you renew your purpose and remain in constant touch with your spiritual self. So dust off those forgotten dreams or aspirations, and strengthen your commitment to making your dreams come true. It will definitely boost your inner and outer self and change your energy level.

Always continue the climb. It is possible for you to
do whatever you choose, if you first get to know
who you are and are willing to work with a power
that is greater than ourselves to do it.

—Ella Wheeler Wilcox

 If you want to learn more about your overall life and determine the current balance sheet of your life, you can download a complimentary copy of the Fit, Fine & Fabulous Life Assessment. www.fitfinefabulous.com

Summary Action Steps—Chapter 10

→ Do you know where you are spiritually?

→ What things do you need to take time to do now?

→ What is your life missing at this very moment?

MONEY OR WEALTH—
IS THERE A DIFFERENCE?

Whathen you become physically and spiritually fit, it makes it much easier to step into your money fitness. A *Strategic Success Plan* must have a financial component for making money and achieving wealth.

When I started writing this chapter, I remembered the VIP luncheon I attended at the Get Radical Conference. Suze Orman was the luncheon speaker. During her presentation she stated, "It is important to leverage self-worth for high net-worth." After her speech, I showed Suze my business card. On my tri-fold business card, it states: "leveraging self-worth for high net-worth."

Suze said to me, "Wow! You really do get it—and don't forget it!"

Suze's Tips for a Great Life

She was one of the most dynamic speakers that I have heard in a long time. Below are some of the tips that she shared:

1. Self-worth does not come from what you look like; it comes from how you feel about who you are.
2. Have faith in yourself and always stand proud.
3. The number one law of money: "Power creates money. Powerlessness repels money and people."

4. For every "no" you receive, just remember it moves you that much closer to a "yes."

5. Credit card debt is bondage. Eliminate it and get out of bondage.

6. Power attracts people, and people control money.

7. Who you are is worth far more than what is in your bank account. Your self-worth has to be equal to your net-worth.

8. You deserve to be treated with respect, honor, and grace.

9. You must keep good company—if they are not good company, let them go.

10. Your thoughts, words, and actions keep you from getting to where you want to be. Your thoughts create your destiny. Your thoughts become your words, your words become your actions, your actions become your habits, and your habits become your destiny. Your thoughts, words, and actions are all one.

Suze's Financial Tips

Below are my favorite recommendations that she shared during her presentation:

- Pay off student loans first.
- Pay off high-interest credit cards next.
- Do not pass up a 401(k) match by your employer. Once their match limit has been met, put the money into a ROTH IRA.
- If self-employed, put your money into an SEP IRA.
- Have at least eight months of emergency funds at all times.
- Everyone must have a will, a power of attorney, and advance directives.

I'm so glad I had the opportunity to meet Suze Orman!

New Year's Resolutions Versus Starting Now

Most people think that the New Year is an ideal time for recommitting to things that are important. So let me ask, what could be more important than being financially fit? What could be better than starting fresh in a New Year? It's very simple—starting fresh NOW!

Now is the time to set your intentions. Here are my picks for the most important resolutions for financial fitness any time of the year.

- Resolve to get started **NOW** on the road to financial freedom. German philosopher Goethe said: "Whatever you can do, or dream you can, begin it. Boldness has genius, power, and magic in it."
- Resolve to write down your financial intentions. You wouldn't start out on a long trip without a road map, would you? Well, the road to financial freedom can be short and sweet (for those who plan and who follow a road map), or it can be a long, meandering path that leads to a dead-end (for those who fail to make a plan to reach their destination).
- Resolve to educate yourself on basic financial planning. Financial planning is not rocket science, and it doesn't have to be boring. The Internet makes educating yourself on financial matters both fun and easy.
- Resolve to stick to a written budget. If you don't have a written budget, prepare one now.
- Resolve to save between 5 and 10 percent of your take-home pay. Don't set money aside only when there's some left over; pay yourself first. There's a good reason why you've heard this advice over and over: it works. Set aside 5 to 10 percent of every paycheck in an interest-bearing account, such as a money-market account, or in a tax-deferred account, such as an IRA.

From the Beginning

I would have given anything for courses on how to start a business, manage money, and attract wealth to have been taught when I was in middle and high school. If these classes had been part of the curriculum, many people would not end up with a mountain of debt and little opportunity to change their fate.

I had to wait until I started my company to learn about wealth and money—but more importantly, to learn the difference between money and wealth.

Understanding Money

Many people think that money is simply cash, but there is much more to money than that. In the age that we live in, most money is never in the form of cash—it's just a bunch of numbers sent by electronic means from one computer to another.

So, what is money? As with most words, *money* can have a number of different meanings. Here's a definition for *money* that you may know: "Money is a medium of exchange." Note that the medium doesn't have to be in the form of notes or coins. This definition means that money is a thing that is used to swap for another thing or service.

Here's a definition of *money* by author L. Ron Hubbard that you probably haven't heard: "Money is an idea, backed by confidence." I love this definition because it fully defines what money is and is not: Money is just an *idea.*

According to L. Ron Hubbard, a hundred-dollar bill is just a piece of paper. If you want to buy something with it, and the person you are buying from is not confident that he can also buy something with the hundred-dollar bill, then it isn't worth anything. It is the *idea* of money and the confidence that people place in it that makes it worth anything.

Understanding Wealth

It may come as a surprise to many of you that money and

wealth aren't the same thing. The dictionary gives a number of definitions for *wealth*, one of which is: "Wealth is having a large amount of money or possessions." This is the definition that most people think of.

But the definition that I would like to propose is much more important to know: "Wealth is the ability to survive a certain number of days forward." This was the definition that I learned when I attended one of Robert Kiyosaki's Creating Wealth seminars.

So how long could you survive if your job ended today?

I don't know whether you noticed or not, but in his definition of *wealth*, money may or may not be important. At the moment, if you have a lot of money, low expenses, and no debt, you can survive for a longer period of time than if you did not have an abundance of money, low expenses, and no debt.

However, during certain times—for example, when Hurricane Katrina hit New Orleans and the people did not have drinking water for five to six days—money may not have helped their chances of survival. But having fresh drinking water definitely would have made a difference.

As humans, one of our prime purposes in life is to survive. Let's get back to that definition of wealth again: "the ability to survive a certain number of days forward." What do you need to survive? You need drinkable water, food, shelter, clothing, the ability to keep clean, and, for the most part, nothing else.

We, as women, have been especially programmed through TV and magazines to spend our money on makeup, jewelry, household decorations, etc. Have a look around at your possessions. How many of them support your survival? It's probably not as many as you might think.

Here are my questions for you: What have you spent money on now that will bring in money later? When will you be financially free and no longer need someone to help you? When will you start to create wealth in your career and business?

According to Robert Kiyosaki, our luxuries should be paid for by our investments. If you don't have any investments, then you shouldn't buy as many luxuries. A luxury is anything that does not directly contribute to survival.

You may need to read this section again to grasp the full meaning of wealth.

Back to Money... Just for a Moment

The money you save should go towards two different kinds of investments: those that create money for you and those that directly support your ability to survive.

What is the Difference between Money and Wealth?

According to Roger James Hamilton, the creator of Wealth Dynamics: "Wealth is what you have left when you've lost all your money." What does he mean? He means that your wealth consists of the things like your passion, your network, your track record, your access to resources, and your knowledge of your industry.

Giving everyone more money does not necessarily result in everyone getting more wealth. Remember, wealth is created when people start trading that money with each other in exchange for more goods and services.

So money changing hands can create wealth, but the act of having money doesn't do it. Some people hoard money to obtain future wealth. This is a bad idea because unless it is earning interest, the money will lose value over time due to inflation.

 Remember, money is a tool and not a typical commodity. Money is *intangible*, wealth is *tangible*. Whereas money is *impermanent*, wealth is *permanent*.

If a wealthy person was hijacked and dumped in a foreign country without money, she would soon be back on her feet because although she might have had her money taken from her, she never lost her wealth.

How many times have you read about wealthy people who lose all their money and then make it back to the top again? This is because they never lost their wealth.

By contrast, somebody who has no wealth, but a lot of money, will soon find ways to lose their money. Lottery winners are a great example of this phenomenon. The US lottery statistics show that within two years, 50 percent of all lottery winners are worse off than before they won the lottery!

This is because although they had money, they were not wealthy, so their money quickly disappeared.

Money is *attracted* to wealth. Money follows wealth, not the other way around. If you shift your focus from making money to creating wealth, you'll begin to see the world in a new light where opportunities to create wealth that attracts money are illuminated all around you.

Before you speak, listen.
Before you write, think.
Before you spend, earn.
Before you invest, investigate.
Before you criticize, wait.
Before you pray, forgive.
Before you quit, try.
Before you retire, save.
Before you die, give.

—William A. Ward

Take advantage of this complimentary Fit, Fine & Fabulous Gratitude Assessment. You just might be surprised at what you will learn about yourself. www.fitfinefabulous.com

Summary Action Steps—Chapter 11

→ What is your definition of money?

→ What is your definition of wealth?

→ Have you distinguished the difference between money and wealth in your life?

GETTING ORGANIZED AND BECOMING MORE PRODUCTIVE

In general, I have found that people do not get or stay organized when 1) stress is not managed, 2) the people in their lives are not organized and consider managing their lives unimportant, or 3) their emotional or psychological problems are not diagnosed and corrected. If these three factors exist, it is difficult to stay focused on any form of organization.

When you have control over these three situations, then you are organized on the inside. When I refer to the inside, I am referring to your emotions, your mental state, and your psychological makeup.

When you are organized on the inside, it frees up energy for organizing your outside. The outside refers to the environment and the situations you find yourself in. We only have so much mental stamina, and if it is all used up solving or managing personal inside issues, little is left over for managing your work, home, interactions, hobbies, etc.

People stay organized in their work and home environments (outside) only when their thoughts and ideas are organized (inside).

Getting Organized

So you have finally decided that you can't stand the clutter and chaos any more. What do you do now? The reality is that getting and staying organized is a manageable, attainable end result if you have the right plan, the right tools, and the willingness and determination to change.

I personally use a proven method developed by veteran organizer Julie Morgenstern, dubbed the "queen of putting people's lives in order" by *USA Today*. In her book *Organizing from the Inside Out*, she suggests these three tips that I simply love (they are very important to organizing from the inside out):

1. **Analyze.** Identify where you are now, where you want to go, why it's important for you to get there, and what's holding you back.
2. **Strategize.** Develop a plan of action and a realistic timetable for reaching your intentions.
3. **Attack.** Methodically sort, purge, and arrange things in a way that reflects how you think.

A. J. Miller, a residential and business organizing expert based in New York City and a past board member of the New York chapter of the National Association of Professional Organizers (NAPO), suggests using the analogy of a small bathroom that has insufficient storage space to apply the analyze, strategize, and attack steps to getting yourself organized:

1. **Analyze and identify where you are now**. Are you frustrated with the small size of your bathroom and the lack of storage space? Are you overwhelmed with duplicates and triplicates of things (you can never find what you need when you need it, so you go out and buy more)?

You should identify where you want to go and why it's important for you to get there: Do you want to be better organized and have less clutter and more storage space? Do you prefer to save time when getting ready and make it easier and less stressful? Do you want to stop wasting money on unnecessary duplicate and triplicate purchases?

Identify what's holding you back from fixing the problem. Do you want more stuff or more space? Are you still trying to figure out where to put it all?

2. **Strategize and develop a plan of action.** If you've got more stuff than space, then either you need to increase the storage capacity of the space, cut down on the stuff, or both. For a bathroom with insufficient storage space and too much clutter in the bathroom itself, keep only those items you regularly use or absolutely need in case of an emergency.

If you buy in bulk, only keep what you need in the bathroom. Non-essential items can be stored in a nearby closet or cabinet or elsewhere. As a rule of thumb, store items at the point of their use; assign every item a single, consistent home; and return it there when not in use.

Make efficient use of all the available space under the sink by using turntables; tiered baskets; clear, stackable shoeboxes; plastic pullout drawers; or other suitable containers. Add shelving or high cabinets to the walls and hooks to the back of the door for additional storage and hanging space. Use appropriately sized containers to hold items so space isn't wasted or items jammed together.

If multiple family members use the same bathroom, consider assigning each person their own tote or container for carrying their personal care articles back and forth from their bedroom to the bathroom. This will cut down on clutter.

You should set a realistic timetable: four to seven hours to sort, purge, and assign a home for items and then "containerize" the items.

3. **Attack based on the plan.** Systematically sort, arrange, and keep items together by category (e.g., dental care, hair care, nail care, grooming tools, cosmetics, medicines, shaving supplies, etc.).

Methodically purge and get rid of expired medicines or remedies you've never used, anything opened and abandoned, and anything old (toothbrushes that need to be replaced, anything that's outlived its usefulness, anything that no longer works properly, anything that looks unappealing, and out-of-date beauty or grooming products).

Finally, arrange and decide which categories will go on which shelves in the medicine cabinet. Don't overstuff them or make items hard to access. Keep only those medicines you use regularly in the cabinet. Save the limited and precious space in the medicine cabinet for those items you use every day. Decide which categories should go under the sink for easy access and which categories should go on which shelves (keeping in mind frequency of use and accessibility). Utilize shelves and hooks without cluttering. Decide which items need to be in or near the shower or bath area, and place them there in practical and attractive containers.

Based on this analogy, you should be able to get organized in every area of your life. It just takes a little time!

Getting Productive

Here are nine great tips for increasing your productivity; select the ones that give you the biggest bang for your time invested.

1. **Eat that frog.** The concept of "eating that frog for breakfast" refers to a time-management concept introduced by Brian Tracy, author and keynote speaker. It is harnessing the energy of getting your least favorite task done first thing in the morning.

   Usually, it is the thing that you put off until the end of the day that drains your energy all day long. By removing that despicable item from your to-do list first thing, you can harness a lot of positive energy, and the rest of your day will be significantly more pleasant and productive.

   Okay, here's my favorite! According to Brian

Tracy, the first rule of frog-eating is this: If you must eat two frogs, eat the ugliest one first.

Here how it works: If you have more than one thing that you have put off and both are draining your energy, do the one that requires the most of you (the ugliest or the worst of the two) first. It will be the most challenging and complex task.

2. **Block time.** Schedule specific blocks of time for your primary duties, important job responsibilities, business-development activities, self-marketing initiatives, social media postings, administrative tasks, phone calls, setting up meetings, etc. The idea is not to schedule 100 percent of your time, but to schedule tasks that are important and urgent.

   Not using a block of time for email first thing in the morning will also greatly add to your productivity. Check your email twice a day—mid-morning and late afternoon.

3. **Determine the one thing you really want to accomplish today.** Ask yourself, "Which one item/task, if I really got it accomplished today, would make me happy, proud, or content?" Highlight the one item, and then do it—try eating the frog for breakfast.

4. **Do your most important work when you are most productive.** Are you a morning person or a night owl? Knowing your best time for being productive will help you determine when you should do your most important work. Doing critical work in your most alert time period will take less time and make you more productive in the long-term. This block of time should be at least two consecutive, uninterrupted hours.

5. **Have a maximum of five things on your daily to-do list.** Most of us, if we would admit it, have a

to-do list that is just too long. According to Verne Harnish, author of *Mastering the Rockefeller Habits*, focus on five—five big items for the quarter, broken into five weekly activities that you further define into no more than five daily tasks or accomplishments. Anything more becomes overwhelming and rarely gets done. For most people, the list may only be three items.

6. **Stop multitasking; it makes you less productive.** Yes—women tend to be able to juggle more things simultaneously, and occasionally that skill comes in handy. For day-to-day business management, however, it can actually make you less productive. Start today by focusing on one task at a time until completion. Then start the next task.

   When you think you are multitasking, what you're really doing is "switch tasking"—switching back and forth rapidly between two or more tasks. There are three consequences of multitasking: tasks take longer, mistakes escalate, and stress levels increase.

7. **Schedule unscheduled time between appointments.** By planning unscheduled time on your calendar and not scheduling yourself so tightly, you are more likely to stay on task and accomplish the things you planned for the day. Unscheduled time allows you to make those in-between phone calls, breathe for five minutes, or take a ten-minute mental break.

8. **Schedule "must" time.** As women, we tend to want to help everyone else first, and then we discover there is no time left for ourselves. It is vital for our physical and mental health that we schedule time for ourselves.

   Whether it's reading, running, being pampered,

watching a movie, or taking that occasional nap, we are totally responsible for rejuvenating ourselves. If we let ourselves become run down and completely exhausted, we are not productive, and it may have a draining effect on the people around us.

9. **Plan tomorrow today.** Jeffrey Gitomer, an author and speaker, frequently says that if you don't know who you're going to call first thing in the morning, you're not in business until you do. Rather than taking the first 15 minutes in the morning to organize or familiarize yourself with your plan for the day, use the last 15 minutes of the day to prepare for the following day.

Your preparation might also include cleaning your desk so you're ready to start fresh in the morning, rather than starting out by feeling overwhelmed by those things that did not get done the previous day. This is the way I stay organized.

Wow! Getting organized and productive is a lot of work. But when you **Re-Emerge** (the third **R** of the 3R Method), what a difference it will make in your ability to become Fit, Fine & Fabulous.

The most effective people do the most
important thing first.

The secret to success is constancy to purpose.
—Benjamin Disraeli

Those who think, plan, and stay organized will reach
their goals and function with great efficiency.

Summary Action Steps—Chapter 12

⟶ What areas in your career, business, or life need organizing?

⟶ What three things can you do to improve your productivity?

⟶ What frog did you eat today?

LOOKING FABULOUS WHILE STORING YOUR WEARS IN STYLE

Image is everything.

We all have approximately seven seconds to make a good first impression. That's the amount of time it takes to shake somebody's hand and take a seat. During that initial seven seconds, you are being sized up.

Did you know that we are judged based on our educational level, our level of sophistication, our attention to detail, how self-confident we are, and our social, career, or business status? The first impression we make is paramount when looking for employment and/or establishing trust with a new client.

With such a limited amount of time to make that all-important first impression, the image you project can communicate far more than your words can say. By carefully managing your image, you can greatly improve the impression you make with others.

In order to have that impeccable image and become a "people magnet," your "attraction factor" is key. Part of your *Strategic Success Plan* is developing a Fit, Fine & Fabulous closet.

How many times have you looked into your closet and said, "I have nothing to wear"? If you hear yourself uttering this statement more often than not, you have a dysfunctional closet. It is probably missing several key pieces that would allow you to easily transition from one outfit to the next. It's time to stop the insanity and get a functional closet working for you.

32 Must-Haves

To begin the process of creating your "attraction factor," here are 32 essentials you must have in your closet:

1. **Black skirt**—it's the benchmark of tasteful, tailored dressing and timeless elegance.
2. **Black jacket**—two- to three-button black jackets with or without matching black pants. It should be a lightweight, seamless material like gabardine or rayon with a small amount (no more than 5 percent) of spandex/lycra to ensure a quality fit.
3. **White dress shirt**—an important closet staple that can be both trendy and classic. Here's a tip: invest in a shirt with just a little stretch in it—it will fit better and flatter any type of figure. I should know; I have five of them.
4. **Black pumps**—you are stepping into the very fashionable legacy of the "gorgeous-heeled" woman of style.
5. **Jeans**—every fashion-forward woman should have at least one pair of great-fitting jeans. Two, five, or ten pairs are even better.
6. **Little black dress**—a closet staple. It should be made of a sturdy but lightweight fabric such as a rayon blend. Avoid heavy wool fabrics that counteract the slimming effects of the color and limit wear during the warmer seasons.
7. **Spandex T-shirt**—black, white, and a bright color

that complements you. These shirts help stretch your closet and are perfect for layering as well as wearing alone. If you have great arms, T-shirts emphasize this asset.

8. **Handbag/tote**—a good quality, hand-stitched bag serves double duty as a briefcase during the week and as a shopping tote on the weekend. Make certain that it has a reinforced bottom, and it should never show wear.

9. **Sneakers**—you need a pair of sneakers that can be worn for working out and casual activities like shopping. I wear Reebok EasyStrides, which are great for walking and working out.

10. **Trench coat**—a classic trench coat can be worn as an all-weather coat and possibly as a dress. I also added a subtle animal-print trench coat to my wardrobe.

11. **Brown/tan pants**—this weekend staple adds diversity to any wardrobe.

12. **Twin sweater set**—the best twin sets are versatile enough to allow for separation in an instant, or you can wear them together as designed.

13. **Leather jacket**—black and brown are great, but why not a pop of color.

14. **Sequined top**—choose sequins that are matte.

15. **Scarf blouse**—this can serve as a swimsuit cover-up and move to evening wear with ease.

16. **Camisole**—your collection should go from under-stated to unexpected to unforgettable.

17. **Lightweight scarf**—some women call them wraps or shawls. A friend of mine calls hers a pashmina, and she is never without it.

18. **Shawl wrap sweater**—a three-quarter length, very lightweight knit creation. It's the best.

19. **Black slacks**—this daily staple is a closet work-horse, a closet stretcher, and a traveler's dream.

20. **Boyfriend sweatshirt**—loose, slightly oversized, and great for lounging.

21. **Yoga pants**—one pair for a healthy workout and one pair for style.

22. **Mules**—they finish a look without appearing too heavily styled.

23. **Chanel jacket**—choose vintage, new, a look-a-like, or Chanel-inspired.

24. **Evening shoes**—your closet is missing real punctuation without a pair of evening shoes.

25. **Evening gown**—the little black dress will not take you everywhere.

26. **Evening bag**—the craftsmanship and finish should make others take notice; make it count, and don't make it match.

27. **Designer leather handbag**—one that complements and accentuates your clothing colors.

28. **Flesh-tone classic shoes (nude)**—it elongates the leg and goes with everything.

29. **Belts**—one skinny and one wide. Be sure to wear it on the smallest point (high or low is very much okay); it makes the old look new.

30. **Pearls**—makes you feel like a lady; wear stacked or mix with a chain (vintage, faux or classic).

31. **Vintage and signature clothing**—every closet should have at least one item for out-classing and out-styling the competition.

32. **Maxi-dress**—it will take you from casual to dress just by changing your shoes and accessories.

Along with your signature clothing, the majority of your shopping dollars should be spent on classic, well-made versions of the above items that fit your personal style.

According to Lloyd Boston, style expert and best-selling author, every woman should have a vintage conversation piece in her closet. He states that vintage clothing and accessories are what separate women who turn heads from women who simply turn to the next hip trend.

Boston also indicates that when all is said and done, your look will be well worth the journey, for no one else is likely to have it and everyone will want to know where you got it—thus its conversation-starting nature. As a curator of your own style, you will now be completely justified in saying, "This old thing?"

What's Not Fit, Fine or Fabulous

1. **Visible bra lines.** Make sure your bra fits properly. If it rides up in the back, slips off the shoulders, or lets your girls sag instead of offering support, then it's time to seek professional help. You can usually find trained fitters in the lingerie area of better department stores.

   Last year, I had a bra fitting at Nordstrom's with Cheryl. She was awesome. I learned so much about the right cut for me, how to put a bra on properly, and where the seam line should fall. Needless to say, my girls are now Fit, Fine & Fabulous.

2. **Roots.** Hair color can do wonderful things for you, but it can also be hard on the budget. If you can't afford the regular maintenance required by all-over color, consider getting highlights instead. Remember, your hair color should complement your skin tone. Most fashion mistakes are easily avoided by a quick glance in the mirror.

   Elaine Stolz, image consultant, identified the best hair and makeup colors for my skin tone. She custom-blends makeup but at affordable prices.

3. **Underarm stains.** First, buy deodorant that

works with your body. You may have to try a few to find the best one for you, and you may need to change every so often if your body chemistry changes: for example, after having a baby, starting a new medication, or going through menopause. If you perspire heavily or need a surefire method to prevent stains, consider using dress shields.

4. **Run-over/run-down shoes.** If your shoes have seen better days, find a good shoe repair shop, and put them in for some TLC. Polish them regularly (I use Weiman Leather wipes for my shoes and purses—I learned this secret from my sister). Be sure to invest in a good pair of shoes if you're going to wear them every day.

   You can use a felt-tip marker on scuffs, and put a piece of soft carpet under your feet when you drive or wear a driving slipper (I never drive in my heels; I wear a soft slipper for driving—it stays in my car).

5. **Broken nails, chipped polish.** Keep your nails clean and evenly trimmed. To make repairs quickly, have a nail file in your purse and at your desk at work. Paint over chips or remove all polish. If you're in a business environment, stick with conservative nail polish colors at work and save the sparkly/neon/funky looks for weekends and vacations. Super-long nails are never appropriate.

6. **Wearing the wrong colors.** All skin tones are not created equal. The lime green, neon blue, or hot pink that you saw on the runway may look fabulous on the models but horrible on you. Experiment with different colors, and stick with the palettes that look best on you, regardless of what's *au currant.*

   You may even want to consider color analysis if you're uncertain which are your best colors. When Elaine Stolz blended my makeup, she also conducted a color analysis and provided me with color swatches that most complement my skin, hair, and eyes. Needless to say, I never buy the wrong color in anything anymore.

7. **Clothing that is too small.** If it doesn't fit, don't wear it. Squeezing into a size 8 may feed your vanity, but it will make you appear overfed to everyone else. Begin to shop by fit, not by size. If you can't sit down or you have to hold your stomach in at all times, you're not going to feel your best or look your best.

8. **Inappropriate makeup.** Light for day, heavier for evening, and sheer for sports or other strenuous pursuits. You wear different clothes for different activities in your life; your makeup should change as well.

9. **Carrying a torn or worn-out wallet.** Everyone should have a leather wallet that is classic in style. A worn-out wallet does not represent success and certainly will not attract money. Every January, I purchase a new wallet for the New Year. What you pull your money out of will dictate what kind of money you will ultimately put back into it. Remember, leather that is top quality usually does not have a gold-embossed stamp that says it.

What Career/Businesswomen Shouldn't Wear in the Office or When Meeting Clients

1. Crocs
2. Fanny pack
3. Sweats (especially if they are frumpy)
4. Tattoos that show
5. Tees (with slogans)
6. What you wore yesterday

7. Flip-flops
8. Too much jewelry (unless you are a fortune teller)
9. Caps (baseball or beanies)
10. Sunglasses when inside
11. More than one piece of animal print

A Closet Meant for a Queen

A few years ago, I had my master closet reconstructed. I even went so far as to purchase wooden hangers. Wow, what a difference they made to the look of the clothes in my closet! I bought them online from a wholesale closet manufacturer, but Walmart sells similar wooden hangers at a reduced price.

When my contractor, Jose G., and I embarked on the project to create a great functional closet, I started with the following premise:

I thought about what kind of things I needed to have in my closet and what could logically go in another place in my home. When we laid out the plan, I considered the capacity of the other storage areas in my home as well.

While Jose G. was busy working on the closet plans (shelves, rods, painting, etc.), I had a big project as well:

- **Sort.** I pulled everything out of my closet and divided everything into categories (e.g., sweaters, dresses, blouses, pants, and jackets). I was surprised by how many of the same or similar items I had purchased.
- **Purge.** I kept only what I actually wore and loved. I threw out clothes that were torn or out of shape. I got rid of the fashion mistakes I had bought but never worn. I gave serviceable clothing to the Dress for Success organization (they have branches in most major cities).
- **Assign.** I then created a specific home—whether

a shelf, section of a rod, or a drawer—for each category of garment (pants and other long clothes on one end of the rod, blouses on the other, shoes on the top shelf, belts on a special shelf).

- **"Containerize."** Now the fun part! I selected attractive containers that represented my style (fashion, you buy; style, you own) to store some items that were seldom worn but priceless. I used shelf dividers to keep sweater stacks from tumbling over. I stored the extra wooden hangers in a decorative basket.
- **Equalize.** I decided to implement a system: "the one-in, one-out rule." For every new garment I purchase, I toss or donate something old to make room for something new. I keep a giveaway box on the garage shelf.

An organized closet will save you much more than time—it will keep you grounded, allowing you to begin and end each day on a note of calmness and help you make a great first impression and a lasting final impression.

How to Dress Fit, Fine & Fabulous without Breaking the Bank

Here are my best tips for not breaking the bank and for maintaining a look that is Fit, Fine & Fabulous:

1. Take an inventory of your closet, and make a list of things you need. Buying from a list will keep you focused and eliminate impulse buying and duplicates.
2. Buy the best quality clothes that you can afford. They'll last longer, wear better, and ultimately save you more money than buying inferior pieces.

3. Buy classic styles. These will stand the test of time and not go out-of-date as quickly as buying trends.
4. Go for mix-and-match separates. If you shop wisely and buy carefully, a little will go a long way. Five well-chosen shirts combined with two pairs of pants will give you ten great combinations versus two head-to-toe ensembles that don't go with anything else and provide only two combinations.
5. Try for a primary color scheme. Build your wardrobe around three to five colors that look good on you. Not only will this allow for more mixing-and-matching, it will reduce the number of accessories that you need.
6. Purchase more solids than prints/patterns. Solids mix and match more easily and are less likely to be remembered than prints.
7. Buy items on sale whenever possible. Also, you may want to visit upscale consignment shops and resale shops; you might be surprised at what you will find.
8. Find a great upscale boutique for buying those super great pieces that enhance any wardrobe. This is also the place to buy one-of-a-kind accessories and outfits.

Remember, every wardrobe should have at least one anchor piece that you build your wardrobe around.

The Attraction Factor

You've got the hair, the makeup, and the outfit all working for you—everything is pulled together. As you journey through your day, you find that you have become a "people magnet." Complete strangers come up to you and start talking to you like you're old friends. This is your "attraction factor." Capitalize on it. It is a great way to get to know people as well as build relationships.

Everyone has at least one "attraction factor." For me it is

my perfume. In the past three years, there has *never* been a day when I have not heard, "What are you wearing? You smell fabulous." This is my Fit, Fine & Fabulous. My second "attraction factor" is my handbag collection. I am known for carrying stunning handbags (to keep your handbags looking great and to maintain their shape, stuff them with tissue paper).

My third "attraction factor" is the compliments I receive three out of every five days: "Your skin is so pretty; what products do you use?" I learned how to implement my Fit, Fine & Fabulous through a skin care regime and custom makeup. I also use another product line recommended by my dermatologist. I absolutely love this product as well.

When you look good, you become a "people magnet"! Studies have shown that even from the cradle, humans are drawn to an aesthetically pleasing appearance. Now here's a secret: you don't have to be drop-dead gorgeous to be considered attractive. You don't have to have the greatest body, the greatest hair, or even a "movie star" face. All you need to do is package yourself attractively, and you'll command plenty of attention. You will have your unique "attraction factor."

Remember: people treat you how you treat yourself. If you take the time to groom yourself appropriately and wear flattering clothes, you're telling others that you're worth the time and effort, that you're important and a powerhouse in your own right. Because you have confidence in yourself, others will put their confidence in you.

A polished image is a powerful tool to have in your success portfolio, so don't be afraid to use it. Remember a Fit, Fine & Fabulous appearance doesn't mean looking like Miss America or the hottest new celebrity. It is looking your best at all times to enhance your career, business or life.

I just thought of another "attraction factor" that I have, which is: I always try to give more than I receive.

Now I want you to take a few minutes and make a list of your "attraction factors."

The Classics

If you want to splurge, stick to the classics—they don't go out of style. For example, purchase a classic Chanel handbag, cashmere cardigan, pearls, Italian linen scarves (they give an extra dimension to your look), diamond stud earrings, a trench coat, and a classic wool coat. Play up one signature accessory, and wear it regularly; you will get more mileage and make a bigger statement from one perfect piece worn regularly than a drawer full of "not-so-greats."

The best advice I have recently read:

> ***Hair:*** To camouflage greasy roots, dust your part and hairline with translucent powder. It's less obvious than baby powder.
> —Amy Sennett D'Annibale

> ***Makeup:*** Use a bronze powder blush all over your face. It helps even out dark skin better than foundation.
> —Kahlana Barfield

> ***Skin:*** Clean your cell phone with antibacterial wipes every morning to prevent facial breakouts.
> —Patricia Tortolani

Just for the Enjoyment

- Fun up your eyes
- Texture up your lips
- Stop fighting frizz
- Rough up a short cut
- Give your up-do a boost
- Glam up your front
- Add a part (front or side)

Don't try to compete with women who are younger
and thinner by wearing clothes that don't suit you.
Great style is based on where you are in your life at
the moment.

—Stacy London, co-host of *What Not to Wear*

Summary Action Steps—Chapter 13

⟿ How organized is your closet?

⟿ Have you identified your personal style?

⟿ Do you have signature pieces in your wardrobe?

FIT, FINE & FABULOUS ESSENTIALS

I am often asked to describe those things that I consider to be essentials in my quest for Fit, Fine & Fabulous. So I decided to put together an all-inclusive list for Fit, Fine & Fabulous toolbox essentials, home office essentials, car essentials, purse essentials, wardrobe essentials, travel essentials, and air travel essentials.

Fit, Fine & Fabulous Toolbox:
- Battery-operated drill and screw bits
- Duct tape
- Gloves
- Goggles
- Hammer and nails
- Level
- Measuring tape
- Masking tape
- Picture hangers
- Pliers
- Screwdriver
- Stud sensor
- Wrench
- Yardstick
- Flashlight and batteries

Fit, Fine & Fabulous Home Office:

- Labeler
- Calculator (three)
- Stapler (two) and staples
- Shredder
- Identity Protector Roller
- Paper clips (all sizes—I love the four-inch ones)
- Index cards (I use them to write reminders and quick shopping lists.)
- Dry-erase board (This is a must. The closet door in my home office is a dry-erase board—yes, the entire door.)
- Bookshelves
- Office supplies (file folders, paper, markers, highlighters, pens, glue sticks, ruler, etc.)
- Storage boxes and decorative baskets (for closets and home office)

Fit, Fine & Fabulous Car Essentials

- Navigation system
- Bluetooth for phone
- AC adapter
- Personal toiletries kit
- Tissues
- Flashlight and batteries
- Golf umbrella
- Flip-flops (in case you want a last-minute pedicure)
- Change of clothes
- Portable office in your trunk (extra business cards, envelopes, stamps, paper clips, stapler/staples, index cards, notepads, etc.)

Fit, Fine & Fabulous Purse Essentials:

- Makeup bag with makeup
- Hand sanitizer
- Altoids
- Lip balm
- Purse-sized tissues
- Cuticle balm
- Emery board
- Loose change
- Eyeglass cleaning cloth
- Whistle on a key chain
- Purse-sized note pads
- Business cards
- Cell phone with an ICE ("in case of emergency") number under your contact list
- Small tote umbrella (I keep it in my car and transfer to my purse in case it looks like rain.)
- Great writing instrument (Mont Blanc or Cross pen)
- A backup pen (I even carry a backup refill for my pen.)
- Index cards (I never leave home without them.)

P.S. Your purse and shoes say a lot about who you are. Invest in a high-quality purse and make sure that it is well organized at all times. The worst thing in the world is to open your purse and have a "multitude of sins" displayed for the whole world to see. You can purchase some great designer bags at Marshall's and TJ Maxx.

Fit, Fine & Fabulous Wardrobe Emergency Kit in a Decorative Box

- Safety pins (assorted sizes)
- Sewing kit
- Baby wipes for deodorant marks
- Miniature scissors
- Static guard to avoid cling
- Tide-to-go instant remover
- Double-sided tape (for an instant blouse closure and to repair ripped hems when in a hurry)

Fit, Fine & Fabulous Travel Kit

- Travel-sized clothing steamer
- Cell phone charger
- Camera
- Sanitizer gel wipes
- Mints (I like Altoids.)
- Baby wipes (great for makeup smudges and for cleaning stains)
- Static guard to avoid cling
- Lip balm
- Small sewing kit
- First-aid kit
- Q-tips
- Duplicate items (miniature-sized facial care, dental care, hair care, and makeup)
- Magic Bullet (use for making fruit and vegetable drinks in the hotel)

Fit, Fine & Fabulous Air Travel Kit

- Entertainment devices (iPod, iPad, or a tablet with headphones to tune out everything)
- Magazines or books
- Nook or Kindle
- Hand wipes (Wipe the arm rests and tray immediately.)
- Tempur-Pedic sleep mask (sold on Amazon) or sunglasses to block out the light if you want to snooze
- Blanket or small wrap
- Ear plugs
- Neck support pillow

I travel by airplanes, trains, cruise ships, subways, cable cars, and cars about ten times each year. I recommend that you avoid dehydrating snacks (salted nuts and pretzels) and drink hot water and lemon (it is usually cold on the plane). Also, when you travel, bring twenty one-dollar bills, and keep a medical emergency card with you. After your stay, it is okay to take the hotel mini-toiletries with you—it is not stealing; they expect you to take them. As a matter of fact, hotels depend on this inexpensive form of advertisement.

Always pack a collapsible backpack. You never know when you will need the extra space. A collapsible backpack has kept me from paying luggage weight overage fees more times than I care to mention.

Six Women, Six Recommendations for High-Achieving Women

I asked six women to define the Fit, Fine & Fabulous essentials that high-achieving women would need for success. Here are their recommendations:

Fit, Fine & Fabulous Essentials #1

Beverly Solomon, Creative Director of Musee-Solomon, indicated that every high-achieving woman should have the following items in her purse:

- An attractive case for business cards
- A nice leather notebook
- A gold pen (It adds a nice touch.)

Beverly was a model and later moved to sales and marketing for such companies as Diane von Furstenberg, Revlon, and Ralph Lauren. Her husband is Pablo Solomon, a recognized artist.

Fit, Fine & Fabulous Essentials #2

Sally Shields, author of two #1 Amazon bestsellers, stated that every high-achieving woman should have the following:

> An iPhone—with it you are sure to never miss an appointment, and you will always be informed of things that could potentially waste your time due to something that is unforeseen. According to Sally: "I was slated to be photographed for *Celebrity Parents* Magazine at 11 a.m. I had a hair appointment set for 9 a.m., but on the way to dropping my kids off at school, I received an email on my iPhone indicating the photographer had an emergency and she needed to re-schedule. Without the iPhone, I would have gotten my hair done for nothing and wasted a couple of hours of time!"

Sally also recommends having cover up, a brush, lip gloss, and a mirror with you at all times. In case you are rushing around like many multitasking women do, it's imperative to always look well groomed. Even if you don't have the time in the morning to perfect the look, you never know whom you might run into, and having beauty items at your disposal will help you make a good impression. Just a bit of lip gloss, a little stick of blemish cover-up, and a makeup brush can make you nearly camera-ready in an instant!

She also says:

> A label maker is a must (one for the home and one for the office). To address envelopes professionally in an instant, I can't live without my DYMO LabelWriter 400 Turbo. It makes professional labels within literally seconds from any address in my database. Invaluable!

> A hot water maker—forget coffee! You can make chamomile or herbal green tea within minutes! Having a nice cup of something hot all day long is wonderful when you are busy and stressing about this and that. Also, without much effort, you can get in your 6–8 cups of water and keep your body nice and hydrated!

> Some pictures of your kids and family. When I'm out and about, sometimes meeting influential people, this is a way to connect. It bonds you almost instantaneously.

Sally is the author of two #1 bestsellers: *The Daughter-in-Law Rules* and *Publicity Secrets Revealed: What Every PR Firm Doesn't Want You to Know*!

Fit, Fine & Fabulous Essentials #3

According to Pat Mussieux, a mindset and marketing mentor, the items, tools, or things that high-achieving women cannot be without, in her professional opinion, are:

- A vision board
- Affirmation cards
- Thank you notes
- A letter of intention

I definitely like her selection.

Fit, Fine & Fabulous Essentials #4

I asked Linda Arroz, former Hollywood stylist, what tools or things a high-achieving woman cannot live without in her office or purse. Linda stated:

> I am reminded of a fun TV segment I did for the Dick Clark's morning TV show, *The Other Half* with Danny Bonaduce and Mario Lopez. The segment was called "What's Your 'Purseonality'?" When it comes to high-achieving women, less is more with the purse. An expensive phone with all the bells and whistles that syncs up her computer and gives her access all the time is essential.
>
> She should have a Skype address. Everyone she knows should be listed as a contact in her address book, and every beauty expert she uses should be assigned a speed dial number.
>
> She should have her secret beauty tool, whatever it may be: most likely a lip-liner, lipstick, and/or gloss. Depending on her age, this beauty tool could be a light-reflecting concealer stick.
>
> Business cards and a pen that doesn't have a promotional logo on it are a must, and maybe a small comb and purse-sized hair products, depending on what part of the country she lives in.
>
> If this high-achieving woman lives in the South, for sure she will have more beauty products and more makeup in her purse than those in other parts of the country. New Yorkers and Los Angelenos tend to scale down and carry only one or two things that give them a fresh lift throughout the day. Carry enough loose change and small bills to pay cab fare, hop on the subway, or to pay for parking.

In her purse (most likely a shoulder strap), she will have something to read at all times, whether it's the newspaper, reports from work that require her review, a magazine, or the latest bestseller. No downtime for her!

In the office, when I was an executive, living a bicoastal, up-in-the-air lifestyle, my office always had the following: a black pantsuit hanging in a garment bag, along with a pair of basic black pumps for those unexpected, last-minute, day-to-dinner command performances, or when the airlines lost my luggage and I was expected to be at work bright and early after a red-eye flight.

A gym bag, stocked with travel-size toiletries, to allow for freshening up during a long, 12+ hour work day, or to take advantage of squeezing a workout of some sort in during the day so you can make it back to work looking fairly put together. This bag of toiletries also doubles as an emergency preparedness kit of sorts.

One desk drawer devoted partly to health with a toothbrush, toothpaste, and assorted OTC/prescription medications needed from time to time. And if this high-achieving woman loves her manicure, her favorite nail polish color is stashed for touch-ups.

Linda Arroz is the owner of Makeover Media, a boutique think-tank specializing in upscale lifestyle, wellness, technology, and entertainment.

Fit, Fine & Fabulous Essentials #5

According to Shannon Mouton, relationship marketing professional, the top ten things that women entrepreneurs, executives, or career professionals should have readily available in their purse, car, and/or office are:

1. Backup phone and batteries; it can be a cheap pre-paid flip phone for emergencies.
2. Mobile phone chargers, one portable and one plug-in.
3. A change of clothes (suit, blouse, and/or dress).
4. Extra makeup; leave what's at home, at home.
5. Additional flash drives.
6. Purse-sized tissues or a handkerchief.
7. Small notepad and several pens.
8. Personal hygiene items.
9. Mints and/or gum, comb, toothpaste, toothbrush, deodorant, and lotion.
10. A pair of stylish flat shoes.

Shannon has a passion for utilizing social technology for building business-to-business and business-to-consumer relationships.

Fit, Fine & Fabulous Essentials #6

One of the best questions to ask Angela Petitt is where she has not traveled, versus where she has traveled. Angela has literally traveled the world during the past three years. So the question that I asked her was: "What things should a high-achieving woman take with her as she travels the world?"

Angela indicated:

> I love the quote "A girl should be two things—classy and fabulous" (Coco Chanel). When I think of this quote, the picture of a high-achieving woman traveling with tons and tons of luggage does not elicit the definition of fabulous!
>
> Those days are gone!
>
> While jet-setting across the continent or cruising the Mediterranean, the high-achieving woman never leaves

home without a pashmina (for those chilly plane rides), a camera, chic sunglasses, a good book or magazine on your reader of choice, your itinerary emailed to someone back home in case of emergencies, and a copy of your I.D. and credit cards in case they are lost or stolen.

Also, a journal is a must-have in order to capture those award-winning ideas and inspirations that come to mind as you open up to the experience of your journey. Most importantly, pack light and have a great attitude ready for a fabulous adventure! Now, you are ready for your trip. Where will your dreams take you?

Angela Petitt, MBA, is working on her doctorate degree and was featured as a 2011 *Essence* Magazine "Power Player."

Take the first step, and your mind will mobilize all its forces to your aid. But the first **essential** is that you begin. Once the battle is started, all that is within and without you will come to your assistance.

—Robert Collier

Summary Action Steps—Chapter 14

⟶ What are your car essentials?

⟶ What are your favorite travel essentials?

⟶ What are your Fit, Fine & Fabulous tips?

YOUR TWO-BOOK PORTFOLIO

Even though I love my iPhone and iPad2 for all the great apps and the ability to keep a lot of needed information—there's nothing like having a "White Book" and a "Black Book." The "White Book" is for my company. I keep the information in this book categorized and sectioned within clear plastic sleeves. This book contains all the important papers and information that pertains to my company.

The "Black Book," on the other hand, contains everything that is important to my personal life.

Here's what's in both:

My "White Book" contains the following:

- Bank account information
- Articles of Incorporation
- Organizational Resolution paperwork
- Company certifications
- Business agreements
- Employer Identification Number (EIN)
- The State's "Good Standing" Certification
- Insurance and bond policies
- Key contacts (i.e., attorney and top 50 list)
- Business-related passwords
- Pricing and contract information

My "Black Book" contains the following information by section (I use white dividers to separate the sections):

- Special Dates
- Family and friends' birthdays
- Special occasion information
- Personal Data
- Personal health and dental insurance information
- Advance Directives and Power of Attorney (copy)
- Credit card information
- Doctors, pharmacy, and dentist contact information
- Service provider's personal information (e.g., hair stylist, manicurist, etc.)
- Alarm codes
- Cleaning service contact information
- Contractor(s) information
- Insurance information (copy)
- Mortgage and property information
- Telephone numbers to remember
- Serial numbers (appliances and equipment)
- Lockbox numbers
- Emergency contacts, friends and family
- Travel Information
- Frequent flyer miles by airline
- Hotel memberships
- Passport number
- Personal Information
- Family members' history data
- My personal data
- Marriage license (if married)

Both books are kept in a fireproof box in my office storage area with cash (in an envelope) for emergencies, backup keys, and blank checks.

Finally, every Fit, Fine & Fabulous woman should have a safe. In my safe, I have a copy of my will (you're never too young to have one), my power of attorney, and advance directives. I have insurance policies, my safety deposit box key, birth certificates of family members, and one of the last cards my mom sent to me prior to her death. I love reading this card.

Summary Action Steps—Chapter 15

➤ Do you have a "White Book"? If so, is it working for you?

➤ Do you have a well-organized "Black Book"? Can it be improved?

➤ What other books do you need to be more efficient?

TAKING IT TO A WHOLE NEW LEVEL: THE PROCESS

"Taking It to a Whole **New** Level: The Process" is the third **R** of the 3R Method: **R**e-Imagine * **R**e-Invent * **R**e-Emerge.

Hopefully, by now you have the beginnings of a functional *Strategic Success Plan*.

In Chapter 4 of this book, I stated that if your *Strategic Success Plan* is designed for you to walk in flats, then tread the course with ease. If your *Strategic Success Plan* allows you to walk in stilettos, don't miss a beat. If your *Strategic Success Plan* is designed for running shoes then sprint the course with grace.

Remember, the key is to always finish what you start, and that means completing all the intentions that are defined in your *Strategic Success Plan*. Then celebrate your arrival to "Taking It to a Whole **New** Level: The Process."

The adorning accessories associated with "Taking It to a Whole **New** Level: The Mindset" are the same accessories you wear in "Taking It to a Whole **New** Level: The Process."

These adorning accessories are classic and timeless, so they will never go out of style. In case you forgot them, here are those classic jewels again:

Setting Intentions
Mastering Clarity
Ensuring Commitments
Practicing Consistency
Achieving Momentum

To master "Taking It to a Whole **New** Level: The Process," you must:

1. Work on your **Intentions**, and master one intention each quarter.
2. Master **Clarity** daily by meditating or take ten minutes to just breathe.
3. Reaffirm **Commitment** as often as needed but always at least once a day.
4. Make **Consistency** one of your daily practices.
5. Maintain **Momentum** because it is your cornerstone.
6. Always "leverage self-worth for high net-worth" in your career, business and life.
7. Soar to "Be the Best and Beyond" (my personal favorite).
8. Enjoy being "on your dime" and "claiming your own exclusive space."

My Personal Trainer's Gift

I wasn't sure how I was going to end this chapter. Then the other day, my personal trainer, Willie E., gave me a video entitled *Facing the Giants*. He said, "You must watch this video and then tell me your thoughts."

At first I thought, "I don't have time to watch a video; I must finish the last two chapters of this book."

All of a sudden I heard a commanding voice: "Now is the time to watch this video." So I stopped what I was doing, prepared a cup of tea, and curled up in bed to watch *Facing the Giants.*

I will not tell you about the plot of the video, but here are my parting words to those of you who are "Facing the Giants" in your life (this 3R Method: **R**e-Imagine * **R**e-Invent * **R**e-Emerge may be a giant for some of you):

Never Give Up
Never Back Down
Never Lose Faith

And you will achieve Fit, Fine & Fabulous!

The best way to predict the future is to invent it.

—Alan Kay

Summary Action Steps—Chapter 16

⟹ Which adorning accessory is the most challenging to wear?

⟹ How can you be the best and beyond?

⟹ How do you know when you are "on your dime"?

THE FIT, FINE &
FABULOUS FORMULA

Even though I have covered all of the components of the 3R Method in the previous chapters, I would be remiss if I did not summarize each of the 3Rs in this chapter.

Summary of Re-Imagine

This is the process of un-writing your life so that you can develop "Taking It to a Whole **New** Level: The Mindset." It sounds a bit backward and a little ridiculous, but it is just what you want to do. The idea of un-writing goes against everything we have been taught in school, at work, and in life.

The reason that Post-it Notes (invented by the 3M Company) are so successful is because people equate writing something down with making a commitment to getting it done. A commitment to change (Taking It to a Whole **New** Level) can start just as easily with a "what-not-to-do" list as with a "to-do" list. In other words, you un-write your past, and **Re**-Imagine your Fit, Fine & Fabulous to create the future of your choice.

Un-writing (**Re**-Imagine) can help you create the story (career, business and life) you want to tell, rather than the one you think you must tell based on where you are today. So when you start to write your *Strategic Success Plan,* it creates the story line (based on your W5 Portfolio) about yourself that you can commit to living and believing with clarity, commitment, consistency, and (please don't forget) momentum.

Walt Disney is the master of Imagineering. Just look at Disneyland—who would ever have imagined such a wonder? Imagineering is the principle of "blue sky speculation," a process through which Imagineers generate ideas with no limitations. The custom of Imagineering has been to start the creative process with what is referred to as "eyewash": the boldest, wildest, best idea one can come up with, presented in absolutely convincing detail. Many Imagineers consider this to be the true beginning of the design process and operate under the notion that "if it can be dreamed," it can be built.

Imagineers are always seeking to improve on their work—what Disney called "plussing." He firmly believed that "Disneyland will never be completed as long as there's imagination left in the world," meaning there is always room for innovation and improvement.

Why not become the Imagineer for the **R**e-Imagine process for your life?

Summary of Re-Invent

This is the process of making over your career, business and life. It is the process of welcoming the new, bringing back into existence some of the old, or recasting something familiar into a different or new form. This is the process whereby you reassess, revise, and regenerate all that you can **R**e-Imagine. Remember you are seeing with "new eyes."

This is the process whereby you restructure your **R**e-Imagine and look at how to repackage your *Why* and your *Wow* so you can walk in your distinctive Fit, Fine & Fabulous.

Here's an example of **R**e-Invent: If you don't have time to go to the gym, **R**e-Invent what a workout means to you. Use light weights at home, stretch and do calisthenics, do a StairMaster-like routine on your second floor or basement stairs. Walk around the block. You can **R**e-Invent your perspective on any intention defined in your *Strategic Success Plan* if you are committed, consistent, and take the necessary time.

Here is another analogy: According to Peter Arnell, author of *Shift*, "Envision yourself as a brand. A company doesn't take a brand 'off strategy' to feel good or to indulge itself. After all, a brand has to be responsible to its constituencies to stay 'on message' and be consistent. But a brand that is not moving forward is a brand that is moving backward. A brand that loses its dynamism risks going belly-up. That's why momentum and forward movement are so important in sustaining the brand that is you."

Without movement, you can't **R**e-Invent, and therefore you have no need to **R**e-Emerge.

Re-Inventing allows you to let in some air and expand your community's perceptions. Some of this can be done through positioning: how you speak about yourself, what you write on your Facebook or LinkedIn pages, how you compose an email or a handwritten thank-you note. Some of it can be done through a "facelift" of you: a new look, hairstyle, clothes, glasses, accessories, etc.

Bring out your best self, and minimize what you don't like. In our world, perception often is reality. Changing the perception will often change the reality.

Joel Osteen, Pastor of Lakewood Church, said: "Pam [cooking spray] keeps things from sticking to a skillet. Why not spray Pam daily in your life to keep things from sticking to you?" This analogy is one of the best ways to **R**e-Invent effectively.

Summary of **Re-Emerge**

This is the process whereby you are spot-on with your *Strategic Success Plan* and you are ready to walk your course in flats, stilettos, or running shoes. It is when you come back into sight or view, or reappear. When you reappear, you are like a new star that just appeared on the horizon. It is the genesis of who you are! It is the debut of the new YOU: Fit, Fine & Fabulous!

Remember, this process is a journey; it is never-ending. Your star shines brighter each and every day as you walk the course.

The Steps to a Life by Design

Re-Imagine
1. Determine the areas in your career, business, or life that need attention.
2. Decide to make a change.

Re-Invent
3. Develop your own life by design plan.
4. Recognize and accept your power.

Re-Emerge
5. Visualize you at a "Whole **New** Level."
6. Share what you have accomplished.

I love AT&T's slogan "Rethink Possible." Isn't it time for you to start to rethink what is possible for your career, business and life?

The 3R Formula

Final Thoughts

The 3R Method is not immediate.

In fact, it is a lifetime commitment, and it is a long-term evolution that you accomplish in small steps, because small steps equal massive success if followed consistently over time.

Along the way you will make some mistakes (at least, I did). Don't be afraid of mistakes. A mistake could turn out to be the best thing that could happen to you. It might turn out to be precisely what you needed to make a breakthrough and gain new momentum.

In fact, remove the word *mistake* from your vocabulary, and rewrite it as a new way of defining *opportunity*.

Remember that Audrey Hepburn quote I shared at the end of the introduction: "Nothing is impossible! The word itself says, 'I'm possible.'"

The Fit, Fine & Fabulous Mantra:

I will never become comfortable with where I am (**R**e-Imagine),
I will always get rid of whatever makes me stop (**R**e-Invent), and
I will always believe and know that everything is possible
and attainable (**R**e-Emerge)!

Let's Review

Many of your dreams may be covered with dust; some of your most precious ones may be shattered and even broken into tiny pieces, while others are conceivable but seem unattainable. You may be ready to implement a change but lack a cohesive strategy. There are some of you who don't dare to dream or even imagine out of fear of failure or disappointment. Don't let anything stand in your way!

For I truly believe that the ultimate "within" is where you move from success to fulfillment to significance. Always look for ways to inspire, inform, and improve at every step along life's journey. Figure out how you want to "show up" in the world, and start showing up in your definition of success.

Fit, Fine & Fabulous is the art of mastering the small stepping-stones of achievement that can position you for success.

Once your "success switch" is flipped, you will find yourself in sync with your Fit, Fine & Fabulous for your career, business and life.

What about the Formula?

I believe that everyone can achieve success and reach their dreams. It is very simple when you follow my *Strategic Success Formula*. This formula is designed to develop and expand your portfolio of success through discovering purpose, unleashing passion, achieving next-level results, and enjoying the realization of your "within."

When you know the formula, it is easy to keep moving. When you have daily tenets, it becomes a no-brainer.

My 10.5 Daily Tenets

Below are my tenets that I follow daily:

1. Develop an exercise regime and stick to it—no matter what (it produces consistency).
2. Send love to someone every day (it could be someone you bumped into at the supermarket; just think about someone different every day, and send them love).
3. Update your *Strategic Success Plan* when needed and follow the plan as written.
4. Quit waiting for Thanksgiving to give thanks, Christmas to give gifts, and Valentine's Day to show and share love.
5. Read (at minimum) one book a month that relates to your career or business.
6. Invest in yourself daily.
7. Make productivity your best friend.
8. Read something inspirational daily.
9. Bookend your morning and night (have a scheduled regime for how you start your day and end your day; everything else will fall into place).
10. Journal daily, and always list three "gratitudes."
10.5. Remember, you can't change what you don't measure—always measure and track your results.

You can't control the length of your life, but you can control its width and depth. You can't control the contour of your face, but you can control its expression. You can't control the weather, but you can control the atmosphere of your mind.

Start your Fit, Fine & Fabulous journey with the end in view. Let your passion pull you forward, and let your *Strategic Success Plan* give you the direction for achieving the success you desire in career, business and life.

Always remember: each and every one of you is born with a Fit, Fine & Fabulous. This book is just a reminder and guide to assist you in perfecting what you already have "within." You have already achieved some of your dreams; now go forward with your Fit, Fine & Fabulous formula to achieve your greatest YOU.

Remember to elevate your enthusiasm, fuel your emotions, fine-tune your focus, protect your priorities, and enjoy the journey.

Always know: eyes may provide sight, but it's the heart that gives insight.

Here are the five things in life I have learned you can't recover:

A stone...after it's thrown.
A word...after it is said.
An occasion...after it's missed.
Time...after it's gone.
A person...after they die.

Life is short. Break the rules.
Forgive quickly. Love truly.
Laugh uncontrollably,
And never regret anything that made you smile.

Enjoy a *Fit, Fine & Fabulous* Life!

Capture Your Light Bulb Moment Now and Keep it Glowing!

Summary Action Steps—Chapter 17

⟶ Do you believe that you have mastered the first "**R**"—Re-Imagine?

⟶ Are you on target for the second "**R**"—Re-Invent?

⟶ When will you complete the third "**R**"—Re-Emerge?

For attractive lips,
Speak words of kindness.

For lovely eyes,
Seek out the good in people.

For a slim figure,
Share your food with those that are hungry.

For poise and grace,
Walk with the knowledge that you'll never walk alone.

Isn't It Time to Make Some
Radical Decisions
And Take Some Drastic Steps?

RESOURCES

Peter Arnell. *Shift: How to Reinvent Your Business, Your Career and Your Personal Brand* (Broadway Books 2010).

Darren Hardy. *The Compound Effect: Jumpstart Your Income, Your Life, Your Success* (Vanguard Press 2010).

Verne Harnish. *Mastering the Rockefeller Habits* (SelectBooks, Inc. 2002).

Steven Harper. *The Ripple Effect* (SWOT Publishing 2005).

Julie Morgenstern. *Organizing From the Inside Out* (Henry Holt and Company 2005).

Cindy Solomon. *The Rules of WOO* (One Plane Ride Publishers 2010).

Entrepreneur's Guide to Capturing the Hearts & Minds of Today's Customers™.

SPECIAL OFFERS

If, after completing all of these chapters, you still have not experienced the transformation you were hoping for... you are still not sure of your direction... you feel that there are still some missing pieces...

If you are still giving excuses such as: "I don't know how... I don't know where to start... I don't have time... Now is not the time... "

In my research, I have found that in many cases when someone isn't getting what they want, it is due to a lack of clarity and direction. Why would there be a lack of clarity and direction? The single most common reason is this: someone is invalidating you or you are invalidating yourself. Sometimes it just takes making some radical decisions.

Whether it is the excuses, lack of clarity, lack of direction, or invalidation, I promise there is an answer in you that is just waiting to come out.

For help in assessing where the stuckness lies or where the opportunities might be, visit www.drlaureen.com and choose one of my many programs: VIP Breakthrough Days, or the Global Association of High-Achieving Women success programs.

Let's take the next step together to flip that obstacle on its head and get you to a point of mastering **G**rowth, achieving **S**uccess and living in strategic **A**cceleration.

Start Living Your Fit, Fine & Fabulous Today

My team and I are here to support you in creating your Fit, Fine & Fabulous life by design so you can live on purpose, make a big difference, do what you love, and ultimately make big profits based on your big passion.

On FitFineFabulous.com

- **Free downloadable resources and work-sheets** that will help you utilize the power of Fit, Fine & Fabulous to succeed in a life by design.
- **Special discounted pricing** is available for bulk orders of the book.

For more information about Dr. Laureen, visit www.DrLaureen.com. Connect with Dr. Laureen and a community of like-minded high-achieving women (and enlightened men) online:

www.twitter.com/drlaureenwishom

www.facebook.com/laureen.wishom

www.highachievingwomen.biz

www.blogtalkradio.com/drlaureenw

Fit, Fine & Fabulous Products

Fit, Fine & Fabulous does not stop with this book. Above are the other Fit, Fine & Fabulous products available to you. Don't forget to take advantage of these free offerings:

Fit, Fine & Fabulous Gratitude Assessment
Fit, Fine & Fabulous Life Assessment

http://www.drlaureen.com

How to Get Connected, Get Noticed, Get Known & Get Paid!

You will learn the method for crafting your "story," obtaining awards and recognition, becoming visible, aligning with your audience, becoming the host at your own event, obtaining more position-based testimonials, and creating an awesome "one-page" for **P**ositioning, **P**lacement, and **P**rofit™.

You will learn the 3**I** Method: **I**mpact * **I**nfluence * **I**ncome™ that Dr. Laureen developed, honed, and follows for building a strong platform and a marketplace presence.

You will discover the system for developing key influencer relationships through integrity, being authentic, and having a recognizable footprint. This system is the touchstone for positioning you as the expert, thought leader, or the "go-to" person.

http://www.drlaureen.com/how-to-get-connected/

Monetizing Your Big Why!

The definition of "monetization" is to use something of value to make money. Your *Why* is your something of value. It is what differentiates you from your competition. It is what allows you to experience **G**rowth * **S**uccess * **A**cceleration™.

This discovery guide and 4-CD series will provide you with the method for establishing your *GSA Factor*™.

The *GSA Factor*™ is a system based on how to determine your *Why* and achieve a life by design that leads to a path for mastering **G**rowth, achieving **S**uccess and then living in strategic **A**cceleration™.

You will uncover the distinction between "owning a business" and "owning a job."

http://www.drlaureen.com/monetizing-your-big-why/

Making Connections, Building Relationships for Massive Results & Maximum Profit$

If you are wondering when you will finally experience a growth in your business—now is the time. If you are tired of feeling misunderstood, undervalued, and seemingly invisible in a more-crowded-than-ever marketplace—now is the time.

If you are confused about what to do next, where to start, or how to take your business to a "Whole **New** Level"™—now is the time to learn how to make connections and build relationships that lead to massive results and maximum profit$.

This CD series is designed for business owners at all levels, but especially for those business owners who want to grow their business and expand their footprint. Now is the time to learn how to make top-notch connections and build high-end relationships so that you can achieve massive results and maximum profit$.

http://www.drlaureen.com/making-connections/

The Ultimate Growth *
Success * Acceleration Package

If you want to skyrocket your career, business and life quickly, you will enjoy having all three of Dr. Laureen's audio and template products to add to your success library. We have even included two bonus books: *Fit, Fine & Fabulous in Career, Business & Life* and *Success Simplified*.

http://www.drlaureen.com/products/

ABOUT THE AUTHOR

"I truly believe that I have been given dreams several sizes too big so that I would have time to learn and then grow into them. Writing this book and experiencing this awesome journey of "getting on my dime" and "Taking It to a Whole **New** Level" has truly been the experience of a lifetime. It was one of those dreams that was several sizes too big when I started writing the book, but now... it is the stepping stone to the next dream that is now several sizes too big."

Dr. Laureen is the CEO and Founder of DrLaureen International, the Global Association of High-Achieving Women, and Masterpiece Solutions, LLC.

She was blessed to receive life's golden ticket—a second chance to grow into her dreams—after she was diagnosed with a major health challenge that resulted in her taking a form of chemo for over seven years and living with the side- and after-effects.

It is her mission to make a difference every day and empower high-achieving women (and enlightened men) to focus on "Taking It to a Whole **New** Level" in career, business and life. Her favorite word is: HOPE—Help Other People Every day.

As an influential **Growth** * **Success** * **Acceleration** Expert, Dr. Laureen inspires high-achieving women (and enlightened men) entrepreneurs, executives, career professionals, and coaches on the importance of "getting on their dime" and "creating their own exclusive space" in their respective marketplaces.

Her sought-after seminars and teachings include those from the High-Achievers' University, the five Breakthrough VIP Day programs, and the success membership programs sponsored by the Global Association of High-Achieving Women.

According to Dr. Laureen, one of the greatest compliments that anyone can give her is to tell her that she is different. When people are different, they make a difference. It is truly her mission and honor to make a difference every day and empower high-achieving women (and enlightened men) toward "Taking It to a Whole **New** Level" in every area of their lives.

If she can help you reach further, leap higher, and achieve greater success, it would be her pleasure to speak with you.

Meet Dr. Laureen and receive free expert training at www.drlaureen.com.